Praying
God's Word
for Your Life

Books by Kathi Lipp

Praying God's Word for Your Husband
Praying God's Word for Your Life

Praying
God's Word
for Your Life

Kathi Lipp

Revell
a division of Baker Publishing Group
Grand Rapids, Michigan

© 2013 by Kathi Lipp

Published by Revell
a division of Baker Publishing Group
P.O. Box 6287, Grand Rapids, MI 49516-6287
www.revellbooks.com

Printed in the United States of America

Library of Congress Cataloging-in-Publication Data
Lipp, Kathi, 1967–
    Praying God's word for your life / Kathi Lipp.
      pages cm
    Includes index.
    ISBN 978-0-8007-2077-3 (pbk.)
      1. Christian women—Religious life. 2. Bible—Devotional use. 3. Prayer—Christianity. I. Title.
    BV4527.L566 2013
    248.3′2082—dc23   2012050785

Unless otherwise indicated, Scripture quotations are from the Holy Bible, New International Version®. NIV®. Copyright © 1973, 1978, 1984, 2011 by Biblica, Inc.™ Used by permission of Zondervan. All rights reserved worldwide. www.zondervan.com

Scripture quotations labeled ESV are from The Holy Bible, English Standard Version® (ESV®), copyright © 2001 by Crossway, a publishing ministry of Good News Publishers. Used by permission. All rights reserved. ESV Text Edition: 2007

Scripture quotations labeled KJV are from the King James Version of the Bible.

Scripture quotations labeled NASB are from the New American Standard Bible®, copyright © 1960, 1962, 1963, 1968, 1971, 1972, 1973, 1975, 1977, 1995 by The Lockman Foundation. Used by permission.

Scripture quotations labeled NKJV are from the New King James Version. Copyright © 1982 by Thomas Nelson, Inc. Used by permission. All rights reserved.

Scripture quotations labeled NLT are from the Holy Bible, New Living Translation, copyright © 1996, 2004, 2007 by Tyndale House Foundation. Used by permission of Tyndale House Publishers, Inc., Carol Stream, Illinois 60188. All rights reserved.

Published in association with the literary agency of WordServe Literary Group, Ltd., 10152 S. Knoll Circle, Highlands Ranch, CO 80130.

To protect the privacy of those who have shared their stories with the author, some details and names have been changed.

Manuscript development by Erin MacPherson

The internet addresses, email addresses, and phone numbers in this book are accurate at the time of publication. They are provided as a resource. Baker Publishing Group does not endorse them or vouch for their content or permanence.

13   14   15   16   17   18   19   7   6   5   4   3   2   1

To my stepdaughter, Amanda. God has wild and wonderful plans for you. It's a privilege to get to watch you become all he's designed you to be. Thanks for the honor of praying for you and getting to see the results up close. You make our lives so much more beautiful and, most of all, fun.

Contents

Contents

Foreword

My husband and I are heavily involved in the missional church conversation, which most of the time sounds like "gospel" but at times sounds like "blah blah blah." (Sorry. I have some church baggage yet to shed.) We're definitely all in, but sometimes all the modern language thrown around by pastor types bogs me down. We've surrounded the kingdom with a lot of rhetoric, strategies, approaches, leadership language, and theology development.

Prayer seems simple in comparison.

Except it keeps blowing our minds and changing the world, so . . .

About two years ago, my husband, Brandon, and I were on the cusp of adoption. We'd put the first two yeses on the table: yes to adoption, yes to Ethiopia. But my pesky husband kept bringing up the idea of two children instead of one. Fear and insecurity got the better of me, and I just couldn't get on board. *Can I handle five kids? Do I have enough for all of them? Can we add two at once to this circus? And, once again, can I handle five kids?*

But he couldn't shake it, and these big ideas are usually in my zip code, not his, so I knew enough to take this seriously. Something was up. And since none of our default strategies and structures could help us, we did the only thing left: we prayed and fasted for a week, asking God to lead us—one child or two?

Our weeklong prayer fast was private; we didn't share it with a soul. On the last day of our earnest seeking, a dear friend called. She knew adoption was imminent for us, but nothing more. Our conversation went like this:

> "Jen, I've been praying for your adoption, and I keep getting this really strange sense. I brought it up to my husband several times, and he finally told me to just call you and ask. If this is off or irrelevant, then just forget it, but I keep getting the feeling when I pray that you and Brandon are considering two children."
>
> At this point, I have stopped breathing. The earth is frozen.
>
> "And again, if I'm getting the wrong message, then disregard this phone call, but if this is true, if you are thinking about two children, we want to pay for the cost of the second child. Whatever the difference is between one and two, we want to cover the entire amount."
>
> (Insert me utterly falling apart.)

As I write this, I'm watching my two Ethiopians jumping on the trampoline in the backyard, tucked safely into their forever family, snatched from the brink of poverty and despair. These two little lives are now a part of our story; none of us will ever be the same. Ben, Remy—they are ours.

God accomplished this through plain, basic, standard-procedure prayer—our friends' and ours. Mysteriously, divinely, he connected us to his will as we came before him in prayer, like he has done with the saints for centuries. Prayer isn't fancy or trendy. It's not "seeker sensitive" or "culturally relevant" or any of those phrases we throw around these days. It is simply connecting with God and his kingdom in the same way as all those who have gone before us: Abraham, Moses, Joshua, Hannah, David, Esther, Isaiah, Mary, Jesus.

When our rhetoric and work ethic and education and intelligence and talent leave us wanting, when they don't close the gap or light the way, we still have the ancient tools God gave us long ago: here is the bread and cup, here is the sacred rest, here is my Word, here are the simple prayers. These help broken humanity, brought together by Jesus, to commune with a holy God—still the most epic miracle in history.

May this book be another tool that sends you to your knees, seeking God in the way he has always been found. His Word is living and active, and our God never sleeps; his ear is always attuned to his children speaking, crying, praising, hoping. May the ancient ways continue to transform us all into true disciples.

Jen Hatmaker, author of
7: An Experimental Mutiny against Excess

Acknowledgments

My biggest thanks go to Erin MacPherson. You are a stretcher bearer in the truest sense.

To the other two authors who have the left side of the stretcher—Susy Flory and Cheri Gregory.

And to the fourth friend who holds me up—Lynette Furstenburg. I am so grateful.

To the kiddos in our life—Amanda, Jeremy, Justen, and Kimber. In every book there are new stories to share. Thanks for trusting me with yours.

Andrea Doering and the rest of the Revell team. Still shocked and amazed that I get to be with you.

To Rachelle Gardner and the rest of the Books and Such team. I'm honored to be a part of you.

To each person who has prayed, encouraged, or held us up this year. We are so grateful. God has used you as his hands and feet.

And finally, to Roger. I have no words, only love. You are the best part of my life, and I'm grateful every day for the man God gave me.

PART 1

Preparing for Prayer

1

How to Use This Book

The idea of praying for ourselves doesn't really jive with the way we women think. We're givers. We nurture others. We hold our friends' hands as they cry. We pray fiercely when our families and friends struggle. We pray, of course. For our husbands, our kids, our friends, our neighbor's cousin's dog . . . but for ourselves? Not so much.

Prayer is life changing. And for women who constantly give—as mothers, as wives, as workers—one of the most powerful things we can do is to pray. In my last book, *Praying God's Word for Your Husband,* I shared stories—both my own and others'—of the hope, hurt, release, and restoration that came from praying for the men in our lives. Now I want to give you the chance to see God move in your own life.

Again for this book, I recruited several women to share their stories about the power of prayer in their lives. Each woman comes from a different place. Some are young, some are old. Some are married, some are single. Some are young career women, others are juggling young children, and still others are empty nesters. But despite the many differences, each of these women has one thing in common: a desire to allow God to do his work in her life. I know from personal experience that if you dedicate yourself to praying diligently—for others *and* yourself—God will move. And move powerfully.

Prayer isn't a one-size-fits-all thing. Whether you're praying over a hot cup of coffee in the morning or desperately crying out to God because of a crisis in your life, your prayers are powerful. I know the stories and prayers in this book will help you to better understand prayer, better understand God's will in your life, and—best of all—allow God to work in your life in ways that you never imagined possible. But before we get started, we need to talk about how best to use this book to facilitate your prayer life.

Getting Through Your Barriers to Prayer

Life is busy. And that means that things—even important things like prayer—can get buried under a pile of to-dos and pushed to the back burner, while life's worries and stresses overwhelm us. Since becoming a Christian, I've known that prayer is important—essential, even—to a strong walk with Christ. But that doesn't mean I've always been diligent to pray.

I'm just like everyone else—there have been times where my prayer life has been "in the zone." I got up a little early, had my list of people and things I was praying about, and got down to the business of talking to and listening to God. I was excited to meet up with God in the morning, and my life reflected it.

And then there were other times.

Times when I woke up and realized I was already twenty minutes behind on my entire day, so I skipped that prayer time and tried to squeeze it into the cracks of my day. And my life reflected it.

Start with a Minute

One minute can change everything.

What is the number one reason you don't have your time with God in the morning?

I know the obvious answer is time, but I think there is a different reason: it's our overwhelming need to do it "right."

I feel like if I can't have a "good" quiet time—one with prayer, meditation, Bible reading, and a devotional reading—then why bother? So I let my overwhelming need for perfection keep me from having a meaningful relationship with God. If I can't take the time to do it right, then I guess I won't do it at all.

I kept thinking that I would have a chunk of time to really do the kind of devotion I wanted. But that chunk of time never magically happened. And my quiet time suffered. Or didn't happen.

One of the things I've learned in other areas of my life is the principle of 85 percent: doing something 85 percent well is about the best I can hope for or expect. It takes the perfectionistic spirit out of things while still giving me something to strive for. My quiet time had become like cleaning my kids' bathroom: if I couldn't do it perfectly, I wouldn't even start.

So I started to apply the principle to my time with God. I would start off with 10 percent of what I thought my quiet time *should* be and work my way up. I figured one minute was better than nothing. I would grit it out and force myself to do more and more as time went on.

What I didn't expect was the subtle way that my heart changed during that 10 percent.

As I started to spend time with God again after a dry period, with just that little bit of time—even one minute—I wanted more. I would tell myself I was just going to spend a minute or two reading *Jesus Calling*, or praying, or reading in 1 John, but I wanted to linger a little. I wanted to go a little deeper.

Eventually, that time became fifteen minutes. Fifteen minutes was a good amount of time: enough to spend some time with God and get my morning right, but short enough that I felt it was manageable. Often I spend much more time than that. But I don't skip it because it's "too much."

If you are wrestling with quiet time, could I talk you into a one-minute quiet time? Does it feel like it would be cheating God? Can I be the one to give you permission to be okay with just getting started? God longs to be with you. One minute will turn into fifteen.

Have a Time

Let's get one thing straight right away: I am *not* a morning person. But I have still made it my routine to pray first thing in the morning. Sometimes I'm bleary-eyed, and sometimes I need a couple of cups of coffee before I can focus, but regardless, I've found that praying first thing in the morning changes the way I respond to life's stresses, worries, and joys for the rest of the day. So it's worth it to me to set my alarm a bit earlier so I can get up and pray.

My friend Annie has young children. She says she used to set her alarm so she could get up early to pray, only to find herself missing prayer time more often than not, as her early-rising kids would pop out of bed the second she turned on the coffeepot. So Annie waits until her kids are off to school or down for their naps before she sits down to pray.

Whether you pray in the morning, at night, or during your lunch break at work, the key is to set aside the same time every day. Pick a time and put it on your calendar with a Sharpie. If you're anything like me, if you don't plan a time, chances are it won't happen.

Have a Plan

You did it. You scrawled the words *prayer time* in permanent ink on your calendar. You're up. You have your Bible. You have this book. Now what?

Making a plan for praying through this book will keep you focused and help you to make the most of your time talking with God. It's a lot like your time at the gym—if you just show up without a plan, chances are you'll end up spending the afternoon sipping an iced mocha in the café. But if you plan—you know, ten minutes to stretch, an hour for kickboxing class, and fifteen minutes in the steam room to finish up—then you're more likely to get the most of your time.

Make a plan that works for you. You can pray through each chapter of this book in order, go straight to your biggest needs of the moment, or pick one prayer from each chapter for your prayer time. You could even use this book in a two-week format, every day praying through a chapter. Whatever you decide to do, just know that choosing to pray—using God's Word for your life—is powerful and will impact you in incredible ways. And that's an amazing, brave, and wonderful thing.

Have Some Flexibility

I don't want to take away all room for spontaneity—after all, I firmly believe that God can and does move powerfully in our lives and we always need to listen to his voice. So write your prayer plan in pencil. Be willing for God to move you through your prayer time. And be willing to listen to his voice when he tells you that you need to spend more time praying for a certain topic or skip over a chapter to get to something that he's trying to teach you.

Have a Spot

Having a dedicated spot to pray is important. It helps you to get in the right mindset to pray. When I sit at my kitchen table in the morning, my brain immediately goes to my Keurig one-cup coffeemaker. Likewise, when I sit at my desk in my office, my fingers almost automatically type in my Facebook password (what can I say, I love connecting with you guys on Facebook). But when I sit down on the chair on my back patio, where I pray on warm mornings (or at the kitchen table when the weather turns cold), my mind immediately goes to prayer. And even when I'm traveling, if I imagine sitting in my trusty prayer chair, my mind goes into prayer mode. It's a powerful thing.

It's so easy to get distracted. Some of us have jobs that take a lot of our time and thinking power. Many of us have kids who need our attention. And our prayer time ends up being piecemeal through distractions.

I want to encourage you to find a spot that's free from the distractions of life. Get away from the piles of laundry. Get away from the kids. Get away from everything so you can really focus.

Have Some Stuff

I keep a prayer basket in the corner of my kitchen that I fill with all the stuff I use to pray so I can quickly grab it and have everything at my fingertips. Here's what's in my prayer basket:

- My Bible. I love *Maranatha! The NIV Worship Bible*. It's out of print, but you can still find plenty of used copies online.

- A notebook that I use as a prayer journal.

- A pen.

- Prayer books. (I love that you're learning to pray for your own life right now using this book.)

- A blanket.

Here are some other books that may help make your prayer time richer:

- My other prayer book: *Praying God's Word for Your Husband*
- *Jesus Calling: Enjoying Peace in His Presence* by Sarah Young
- *Life of the Beloved: Spiritual Living in a Secular World* by Henri J. M. Nouwen
- *Celebration of Discipline: The Path to Spiritual Growth* by Richard J. Foster

Have No Fear

Confession time. I used to worry that God wouldn't think my prayers were good enough. As though if I didn't say the right things at the right time with the right scriptural references woven into my words, he wouldn't listen. Have you ever felt that way? As if the words of your heart were entirely too insignificant for our great big God to even pay attention to?

Psalm 147:11 says that the Lord delights in those who put their hope in his unfailing love. *Delights*. And that means a simple, heartfelt prayer—a prayer where you hand your hopes, your fears, your worries, and your cares over to God—will be delightful to him. He longs for us to be personal with him—to cry out to him in conversation, to share who we are and who we want to become.

I want to encourage you to let go of your fears—of inadequacy, of insignificance, and of doing things "wrong"—and just pray. Pray from your heart in a way that could never be rehearsed or perfected; simply let him see you. One tool I've found useful in doing this is to use God's Word as a guide when I pray (which is why I wrote this book and *Praying God's Word for Your Husband*). You don't have to pray a certain way or be fearful that if you deviate from Scripture, God won't listen, but having Scripture at your fingertips when your soul is crying out to the Lord will give you the freedom to share your heart with the one who cares most.

Going Beyond Quiet Time

Praying changes you. And that's why I encourage you to pray every day. Continuously. Pray for every person in your life, every situation in your life, and every trial in your life. Pray in your minivan as you drive your kids to soccer practice. Pray during your lunch break at work. Pray in the middle of the night when you wake up and can't get back to sleep.

I think a lot of women get into a quiet-time box. They set aside time to pray and have a routine (both good things), but they have difficulty expanding their prayer life beyond that.

Here are a few ways you can pray outside the box.

With Your Husband or a Friend

How often do you pray with someone else? Some of you may say every day (a great thing), and others may say never. Regardless of where you are, I think sharing this book and your prayers for your life with your husband or a trusted friend will not only strengthen your relationship, it will also strengthen your prayer life.

So invite someone else into your prayer life. Share with them what you're praying for and ask them to join you in petitioning God.

In a Crisis

There are times in every woman's life—times of trial, crisis, and despair—when even praying feels overwhelming. Of course, these are the times when it's most important for you to pray. I encourage you to dig deep into Scripture and pray through your despair to find God's hope and encouragement. In situations like these, I recommend you turn to certain chapters to find prayers that are targeted toward times of crisis: chapter 4 ("When You're Overwhelmed"), chapter 9 ("When You Feel Inadequate"), and chapter 13 ("When You're Despairing").

And don't be shy! When you are in an emergency, people want to help but don't know how. Give them the verses and the prayers to pray and then ask them—or beg them—to intercede on your behalf.

2

Preparing Your Heart to Pray

When my daughter Kimberly was five, she was a bona fide prayer warrior. She'd fold her hands and close her eyes tight and then earnestly cry out to God with the most longing, loving, and earnest prayers I'd ever heard. She'd thank God for his incredible love, she'd rave about the beauty of his creation, and then she'd remember in depth the needs and wants of each of her friends and family members. It was beautiful, and more often than not, I'd leave her room teary-eyed and in awe of her pure, childlike faith.

Back then, my prayer life stood in stark contrast to hers. Sure, I prayed. Especially for my kids. But it was more the expected "thanks, God, for everything you do for me" than a passionate, sincere, and deep relationship with God.

I'd brew a cup of coffee, open my Bible, read a verse, drink half of the coffee, say a quick prayer, refill my coffee, pray for my kids, drink more coffee . . . and before I knew it, a half hour would've passed and I'd have hardly spent any time praying in earnest.

But that all changed.

At first, I found myself praying for everyone but me. I prayed for my husband, Roger, I prayed for my kids, and I prayed for a long list of other people in my life.

Then, after a period of time when Roger and I were both dealing with our own crises on opposite sides of the country and couldn't be together (and had a hard time connecting by phone with the three-hour time difference), I started to pray Scripture for my husband.

And the crazy thing was, it worked. I saw God restore peace to Roger's life. I saw Roger walk with a new confidence. I saw him deal with family situations with extra patience and grace. And I realized that this praying Scripture stuff works.

With few expectations, I tried it for my own life. And the results were amazing. I finally had a consistent prayer time. I saw changes not just in myself but in my circumstances. Things the world would have called coincidences, I now saw as God directly intervening in my life.

Maybe you aren't as bad as I was. Maybe you have gotten into a rhythm where your prayer life is consistent and powerful and sincere. That's great. Or maybe you never pray at all. Maybe you have never gotten into the habit, and the reason you picked up this book is that you want to change that. Regardless of where you are, lots of things can stand in the way of prayer. Here are a few of the common obstacles and how you can overcome them.

Time

You're busy. I get that. And for a lot of women, twenty-four hours is just not enough time in any given day to get everything done. But I want to encourage you—no, *urge* you—to set time aside for God. I think you'll find (as I did) that when you give your time to God, he in turn multiplies your time, your energy, and your gifts. There is nothing better you can do with your time—not work, not volunteer at church, not parent—than build your relationship with your heavenly Father. So while it may seem next to impossible to fit another to-do on an already bursting list, I want to encourage you to do exactly that.

Practical Steps

- Like I said in chapter 1, set aside a specific time every day to pray.
- Put a reminder on your phone. Every morning at 7:00 on the dot, I have a little message that pops up and says, "Time for quiet time, Kathi!"
- Set a timer. I know that sounds very authoritarian, but when I set a timer and dedicate a time to praying, my mind is able to stay focused on the task at hand instead of wandering to other things.

Everyday Distractions

You sit down to pray, and just as you close your eyes, the dog whines to be let out. You settle back down, but five minutes later the phone rings. Then a text message comes in. Then the kids want a snack. Does this sound familiar? During prayer time, it's so easy to get distracted by . . . well, everything but praying.

Practical Steps

- If you have young kids, ask your husband or a friend or even Mr. TV to watch them while you pray. Take it from someone who knows—if you attempt to pray while your kids play "quietly" in the other room, you're going to end up spending more time telling them to go back into the other room and play quietly than you will praying.

- If it's at all possible, pray when you're alone. I remember a time when I literally sat my kids down in front of the TV, went outside and sat in my car, and *locked the doors* just so I could get a few minutes to pray. (The kids were in my line of sight the whole time.)

A Wandering Mind

Even when I am able to push away everyday distractions and find a quiet time and place to pray, I find that my mind often wanders. I'll have every good intention of spending my time praying, but then I'll start thinking about a project I'm working on or a conversation I've had with Roger, and before I realize what's going on, my mind will have gone down this long, extended rabbit trail, and I won't even remember what I was praying about to begin with.

Practical Steps

- This probably sounds very teacher-ish of me to say, but focus is a habit of the mind. That means the more you practice staying focused, the better you'll get at it.

- Use a guide (like this book) to help you stay on track. I find when I sit down and say I'm going to just pray, my mind ends up wandering. But if I sit down with the intention of praying for something specific—my family, my kids, my finances, my relationships—I am able to stay on track.

- Pray that God will help you stay focused as you pray. Sounds simple, but hey, it works.

- When my mind is really scattered, I will "breathe" prayers to quiet my thoughts and connect to God. I will close my eyes, breathe in, and pray a two- or three-word prayer— "You are here" or "I praise you"—and then exhale.

Unreasonable Expectations

Confession time. There have been times (once or twice) in my life that I've gotten completely wrapped up in reality TV shows. I get my heart set on Mr. Adorable-with-the-Gorgeous-Voice winning *American Idol* and then showing up at my church to play a special concert just for me before he's whisked off on his worldwide tour. But then he gets kicked off the show. And I find out that he's not quite as adorable as I thought. Suddenly I'm mad at the judges for ruining my fun and mad at the network for putting me on such an emotional roller coaster. Did I mention that I tend to get wrapped up in reality TV?

But I digress. My point is that sometimes we look at praying as a magic cure-all to all of life's woes. Then when life doesn't turn out exactly like we planned it, we get mad at God. And we stop praying. But that's completely backward from the way God intended prayer. He created prayer as a means for us to build a relationship with him. It's our way to seek him—his counsel, his will, his ways—and not our way to get what we want.

Practical Steps

- Pray not only to petition God but also to honor him, express gratitude, and build a relationship with him. When we look at prayer as a relationship instead of a means to an end, our resistance disappears.

- Write down your prayer requests in a dated journal. Whenever you start to doubt God's sovereignty, go back and look at some of your old journals. I've done that and found that over time, God's answers to my prayers—whether affirmative or negative—are always what I needed at the time.

3

Why Pray This Way?

Using this book to pray is by no means the only way to pray. It's not even the only way I pray. I am just one person—a regular mom and wife without a fancy seminary degree—and while I have cracked the code on how to make the best chicken poppy seed casserole west of the Mississippi (the recipe can be found at www.KathiLipp.com), I have not cracked the code on how to pray perfectly.

But this book is a tool that you can use to make your prayer life better and stronger. Praying Scripture is something that I have found works for me for many reasons, so I want to share it with you.

＊

Reason #1: God Asked You to Pray

Be joyful in hope, patient in affliction, faithful in prayer. (Rom. 12:12)

Sometimes we should just do things because God tells us to.

My daughter Kimber was my "why, why, why, why, why" child. If I asked my kids to run and put on their shoes, Justen would go put them on. But Kim? She'd ask why. "Why do I need shoes on? And why do we need to wear shoes anyway? And why do I have to do it now?" Why, why, why, why, why.

But I can't complain too much because Kimberly got her why-why-whying from me. I also want to know why. Why do you put baking soda instead of baking powder in cookies? And why is my Keurig able to brew one perfect cup of coffee in less than thirty seconds when the little machines in hotel rooms can't brew anything better than brown water, no matter how many times I try? I just want to know.

So with all that in mind, I'm sure you can imagine how well it went over when I tried the quintessential "do it because I said so" line with Kimber. Let's just say I learned really quickly to always—always—give her a real answer.

All that said, I've learned as an adult that there aren't always cut-and-dried answers for things. Some things are just the way they are—and that is especially true when it comes to God. Being a Christian takes faith, which means not always asking why when God tells us to do something.

So when God says, "Pray faithfully," I've learned to say, "Yes, God" instead of "Why, God?" There are lots of reasons to do things, but probably the most important one is because God told us to. And he knows better than we do.

Reason #2: God Wants to Know You

I love those who love me,
and those who seek me find me. (Prov. 8:17)

God loves you. He always has, always will. And because of his incredible love for you, he wants to know you. And not just on a shallow level—he wants to know everything about you. Every thought. Every worry. Every joy. Every sorrow. Every sin. Every battle. *Everything*. And that's a good thing.

Also, God loves those who seek him. How's that for incentive to seek God through prayer? 😊

The reason that praying Scripture works so well is that not only does it give you a framework with which to seek God, but as you allow him to know your heart, your mind, and your soul on a deeper level, you're also learning about him through his Word. I think you'll find that the more you pray this way, the more you'll want to pray this way, because it really enriches your relationship with the Lord.

Reason #3: God Has Given You All You Need for Life and Godliness

His divine power has given us everything we need for a godly life through our knowledge of him who called us by his own glory and goodness. (2 Pet. 1:3)

Since I'll be baring my soul to you guys throughout this book, I might as well get it all out in the open right from the get-go.

So here goes. There are times—lots of times—that I check in with Facebook in the morning before I check in with God.

Like I said before, the time I've set aside to pray is first thing in the morning. I'll get all set to pray, but then I'll catch a glimpse of my laptop leering at me across the room. And I'll take a quick break from my quiet time to check one teeny-tiny thing. And one teeny-tiny thing turns into two medium-sized things, and before I know it, I'm reading an article about Jessica Simpson's choice of baby names instead of having my quiet time. Whew. How's that for soul baring?

We live in the information age! Between Google and Pinterest and blogs and instantly downloadable ebooks, it's easy to start thinking of the Bible as when-I-have-time reading instead of essential reading.

But God told us that he has given us everything we need for life and godliness in the Bible. Which means—don't hate the messenger—Facebook is not an essential source of information.

Don't get me wrong. I'm not telling you to stop reading anything that's not in the Bible. I'm simply saying that God's Word is rich and powerful and leads to wisdom that goes far beyond that which you can find on Google. And by praying God's Word for your life, you're giving him the opportunity to weave his truth into every area of your life.

Reason #4: God Wants to Give to You Abundantly

I have come that they may have life, and have it to the full. (John 10:10)

I like to call it "more Christmas syndrome." And I feel like I probably have earned the right to name it, because I have suffered from it every year for at least twenty years now.

It works like this: I set a Christmas budget, I look online to figure out what I want to get every family member, I shop around for the best prices, I clip coupons, and I find deals. I make my plan to purchase the things I need, I wrap everything in pretty paper, and I put it all under the tree. And then I step back and admire the glory, anxiously awaiting the fun of Christmas morning when my kids will tear open the presents.

But then I see an ad with a really cool gadget that I know Roger would love.

Or I spot a pair of jeans in a shop window that Kimber would absolutely die for.

And even though I've already spent my entire Christmas budget on carefully selected gifts for each family member that I know they will love, I want to buy more.

God is kind of like that. He has already given you all of the best gifts—eternal life, hope in Christ, his Word to guide you—yet he wants to give you more. He wants to give to you in abundance. All you have to do is ask.

Reason #5: God Answers Prayer

Ask and you will receive, and your joy will be complete. (John 16:24)

God answers prayer. He answers prayer.

It's simple. It's profound. It's a bit baffling to think that the Author of life listens to our prayers and answers them. But he does. It says so in the Bible over and over.

And because God answers prayer, it should be our priority to pray.

PART 2

Prayers for Your Life

4

When You're Overwhelmed

Character cannot be developed in ease and quiet.
Only through experience of trial and suffering can
the soul be strengthened, ambition aspired, and
success achieved.

Helen Keller

We women are master multitaskers. We can talk on the phone while simultaneously folding laundry and planning next week's dinner menu. We can do the dinner dishes while planning next summer's family vacation. We can put on mascara while ironing our hubby's dress shirts and eating a soy-flax yogurt parfait.

But even for the woman who can do it all, life can be overwhelming.

There are just those days (or months) when everything comes crashing down on you. When the soy-flax yogurt parfait falls on your freshly mopped floor. When the laundry starts to pile up. When your to-do list is longer than your teenager's "every kid in the entire universe has unlimited texting on their phone except me" rant.

Unfortunately, there are very few people who can drop everything and head to the spa for a mani-pedi every time life gets overwhelming. So what do you do when life throws you an overwhelming curveball? You know what I'm going to say, don't you? You pray.

When You Have Too Much to Do

There was a time in the spring of 2011 when I could've worked forty-eight hours a day, fourteen days a week, and still wouldn't have finished half of the things on my to-do list. I had one book deadline looming, another book needing edits, three weekend retreats that I was speaking at, and a major convention to prepare for. Suffice it to say I was a bit overwhelmed (and let's not get into how Roger spent two weeks hiding out in the den, eating chips and salsa and avoiding interaction with stressed-out Kathi).

Interestingly, as my stress level rose, my capacity to pray declined. I desperately needed God's intervention, yet the more I added to my to-do list, the less I turned to the one who could relieve my stress.

When we're weighed down with mile-long to-do lists, and the burdens of parenting, work, marriage, and housekeeping seem too much and too big, God is there. And while he may not shorten our to-do lists, <u>he can and will come beside us and help us carry the burden</u>.

Praying God's Word When You Have Too Much to Do

Then Jesus said, "Come to me, all of you who are weary and carry heavy burdens, and I will give you rest." (Matt. 11:28 NLT)

Lord, I am tired. My burdens are heavier than I can bear. Lord, please give me rest.

Take my yoke upon you. Let me teach you, because I am humble and gentle at heart, and you will find rest for your souls. For my yoke is easy to bear, and the burden I give you is light. (Matt. 11:29–30 NLT)

Lord, you've promised if I ask, not only will you take my burdens upon you, but you will teach me how to find rest for my soul. My soul craves that right now— yet everywhere I turn I find something else to worry about. Lord, show me your ways. Fill my soul with your gentleness today.

Search me, O God, and know my heart;
    test me and know my anxious thoughts.
Point out anything in me that offends you,
    and lead me along the path of everlasting
        life. (Ps. 139:23–24 NLT)

Lord, you don't desire for me to be anxious. Instead, you want to sanctify me through the work that you have given me to do. Search me. Show me what I'm doing that is ungodly, and help me to remove it from my life so the work I do will be for your glory alone.

For I am the LORD your God
    who takes hold of your right hand
and says to you, Do not fear;
    I will help you. (Isa. 41:13)

Lord, thank you for holding my hand when I am over-whelmed. Please reveal yourself to me in new ways today. Fill my heart with your comfort. Fill my body with your strength and my busy day with your rest. Help me to trade my worry and my stress for complete reliance on you. Every time I start to feel overwhelmed, fill me with the peace of mind that comes with the knowledge that you have promised my soul rest.

When Work and Life Don't Seem to Balance

I love my job. I love meeting women at speaking events, laughing with women from all walks of life, sharing my story, and (hopefully) inspiring people to love God more and love their families better. Loving my job is a good thing—I'm blessed— but there are still times when work infringes on my personal life and I'm left feeling completely out of balance.

When work seems to be spilling into the time you have with your family—when family dinners are interrupted by work phone calls, and when your mind is whirring with thoughts of work even when you should be doing other things—turn to the Lord. Turn to the one who understands what it is to tarry, who always made time for the ones he loved, and who knew the importance of rest.

Praying God's Word for Balance in Work and Life

As Jesus and his disciples were on their way, he came to a village where a woman named Martha opened her home to him. She had a sister called Mary, who sat at the Lord's feet listening to what he said. But Martha was distracted by all the preparations that had to be made. She came to him and asked, "Lord, don't you care that my sister has left me to do the work by myself? Tell her to help me!" (Luke 10:38–40)

Lord Jesus, like Martha and Mary, I feel torn. I am
pulled in many directions. Help me to discern how to
balance my time, my energy, and my resources so I can
be my best for you, my family, and myself.

"Martha, Martha," the Lord answered,
"you are worried and upset about many
things, but few things are needed—or indeed
only one. Mary has chosen what is better,
and it will not be taken away from her."
(Luke 10:41–42)

Father God, I want to choose the better path—the path
that leads me closer to you and your will in my life.
Show me what warrants my time, energy, and attention,
and what can be pushed aside.

It is useless for you to work so hard
    from early morning until late at night,
anxiously working for food to eat;
        for God gives rest to his loved ones.
            (Ps. 127:2 NLT)

Lord, you tell us that those who work hard will prosper
(Prov. 13:4), yet today I feel like my work is overtaking
my life. I need balance. Help me to manage my time so I
can focus on what matters most, when it matters most.

From the end of the earth will I cry unto
thee, when my heart is overwhelmed:

lead me to the rock that is higher than I.
(Ps. 61:2 KJV)

Father, no matter how unbalanced my life feels, you are my rock. You are a tower of refuge that will help me find the balance I need and crave. Lead me as I work to align my will with yours.

When Life's Trials Get Overwhelming

Remember how I told you about the time in my life when I was feeling weighed down with book deadlines, speaking preparations, and editing projects? What I didn't tell you was during that time, I was also facing some of the biggest trials of my life. My mom had been diagnosed with a particularly devastating form of cancer and was facing major surgery, my relationship with my son Justen was floundering, and as if that wasn't enough, I was diagnosed with whooping cough after weeks of feeling utterly drained.

Have I mentioned that I was a little bit overwhelmed? My body went into survival mode—every ounce of energy I had was being thrown into just surviving. But when I turned to the Lord in prayer, something powerful happened. No, he didn't immediately lift my burdens (though he has since healed both my mom and me and restored my relationship with Justen), but he did fill my soul with a peace that defied understanding. He filled my empty spaces with his grace, giving me the energy and the drive to keep trudging through the mire. What a powerful God we serve!

Praying God's Word in Times of Trial

> Your righteousness, O God, reaches to the
>   highest heavens.
> You have done such wonderful things.
> Who can compare with you, O God?
>   (Ps. 71:19 NLT)

Lord, I am being tested right now. Life feels utterly hopeless, yet I am reminded that your righteousness is bigger and wider and deeper than my troubles. Your love reaches to the highest heavens and to the depths of my pain. You have done wonderful things. Nothing compares to you, Lord.

> You have allowed me to suffer much
>   hardship,
>   but you will restore me to life again
>   and lift me up from the depths of the
>   earth. (Ps. 71:20 NLT)

I'm suffering right now, Lord. I feel lost and alone. I am struggling to put one foot in front of the other and keep moving forward in this world. Lord, please comfort me. Remind me that you will restore me to peace and life again. This pain will end. My hope will be restored. And when it does, you will still be God.

You will restore me to even greater honor
and comfort me once again.
(Ps. 71:21 NLT)

*Your promises are music to my soul right now. I can
trust you to bring me comfort in my time of trial. Fill
me with the peace that comes from knowing that your
promises of restoration and hope will come to fruition
in my life.*

Practical Steps

Praying is probably the most important thing you can do
for yourself when you're overworked and overwhelmed. But
what other practical things can you do when stress is taking
over your life? Here are some simple, ten-minute sanity sav-
ers for you.

- Every time you check a task off your to-do list, allow
  yourself to watch ten minutes of fun TV (there is no
  shame in obsessing over *Dancing with the Stars*) or read
  ten pages of a novel.

- Call your husband and ask him to pray with you.

- Cross unnecessary tasks off your to-do list. Skip the grocery shopping, order in pizza, and give yourself permission to focus on tasks that are truly nonnegotiable.

- Go outside and play with your kids for ten minutes.

- Read an uplifting psalm. (Hint: Go to www.biblegateway.
  com and do a keyword search for *peace* or *rest*.)

- Put something fun on your iPod (Carrie Underwood, anyone?), turn it up, and sing along.

- Treat yourself to something indulgent and yummy— dark chocolate, a nonfat vanilla latte with whip, an apple dipped in caramel sauce.

- Go on a short but brisk walk around your block and think about anything and everything except your to-do list.

- Laugh.

- Call a friend—just for fun.

- Spend ten minutes throwing a ball to your dog or snuggling with your cat.

- Rub on some aromatherapy lotion, (I love the Japanese Cherry Blossom scent from Bath & Body Works.)

5

Your Relationship
with God

Nothing can separate you from God's love, absolutely nothing. God is enough for time, God is enough for eternity. God is enough!

Hannah Whitall Smith

God loves you.

Roll that around in your mind for a second.

God, the Creator of the entire universe, created you. The Author of life chose you to be his treasured, adopted daughter. The one who has numbered the stars in the sky has also numbered the hairs on your head. And he desires a personal relationship with you. I love that.

But how can I—wholly flawed, wholly human, and wholly insignificant—get personal with an all-knowing, all-powerful God? Seems a little bit, um, presumptuous to sit down and ask him to spend his time getting to know me.

Amazingly, God calls us to do exactly that—to share a deep and meaningful relationship with him. One of the best ways to strengthen that relationship is through prayer. So as you read this chapter, I want to encourage you to sincerely seek him, drawing close to him through prayer, through meditation, and by reading his Word, so you will know him better—for no other reason than for the fact that he loves you.

Praying God's Word When You Need to Draw Close to Him

I have loved you with an everlasting love;
I have drawn you with unfailing kindness.
(Jer. 31:3)

Father God, I draw so much comfort from the fact that your love is everlasting. There is nothing I can do or say that will separate me from you. I recognize that I don't deserve your unending love. Yet because of your unfailing kindness, you offer it willingly. You've invited me into a personal relationship with you, and I accept. I want to know you better.

He tends his flock like a shepherd:
He gathers the lambs in his arms
and carries them close to his heart;
he gently leads those that have young.
(Isa. 40:11)

52

Jesus, you are the Good Shepherd. Pull me into your arms. Draw me close to you and help me to live every moment of my life wrapped up in your everlasting love. I know I am not strong enough, not big enough, not good enough to cling to you, so cling to me, Jesus.

Your love, LORD, reaches to the heavens,
    your faithfulness to the skies.
Your righteousness is like the highest
      mountains,
    your justice like the great deep. . . .
Continue your love to those who know you,
    your righteousness to the upright in heart.
      (Ps. 36:5–6, 10)

Holy God, your ways are bigger and better than I can even comprehend. But I want to understand you better. I want to feel your love, to see your faithfulness, to learn from your righteousness, and to experience your justice. Lord, my heart is willing. Teach me your ways.

As the deer pants for streams of water,
    so my soul pants for you, my God.
      (Ps. 42:1)

My soul craves you, Lord. I want more of you in my life. Give me the courage to give myself wholly to you so I can know you better.

Praying God's Word for Your Prayer Life

Pray to God and find favor with him,
  they will see God's face and shout for joy;
  he will restore them to full well-being. (Job 33:26)

Wow, Lord, there is such power in prayer! Lord, I want to see you clearly. I want to see who you are, what you desire, and what your plans are for my life. Create in me a desire to pray wholeheartedly, continuously, and faithfully.

Praise awaits you, our God, in Zion;
  to you our vows will be fulfilled.
You who answer prayer,
  to you all people will come.
When we were overwhelmed by sins,
  you forgave our transgressions.
Blessed are those you choose
  and bring near to live in your courts!
We are filled with the good things of your
    house,
  of your holy temple. (Ps. 65:1–4)

God of Zion, it is a great privilege to serve a God who desires a personal relationship, and I praise you for drawing me close to you through prayer. Lord, I am a sinner—I fall short of your glory every day, every hour, yet you have forgiven me. I humbly desire to know you better, to live in your courts, and to be filled with the good things you have promised.

But I pray to you, LORD,
  in the time of your favor;
in your great love, O God,
  answer me with your sure salvation.
Rescue me from the mire,
  do not let me sink. (Ps. 69:13–14)

Lord, you have given me so much! I am in awe of your great love—of the fact that you have given me a promise of sure salvation. What wonderful consolation! But there are times I feel like I am sinking—when the worries and trials of this life are overwhelming me. Rescue me, Lord! Do not let me sink. Teach me to turn to you, my Savior and Rescuer, in good times and bad.

When You Can't Comprehend His Ways

I'm starting to think that my three-year-old, Haddie, isn't catching on to the ins and outs of the concept of maturation: "Mom, when I grow up and Daddy grows down, will he be my baby?" and "When you're a baby again, can I put you in time-out?" and "When Nana gets to be a little girl, will she be crawling?"

No matter how many times we have explained that people only grow one way—up—the same questions keep coming. Haddie is adamant that if we grow up, we should eventually start growing back down at some point. Her three-year-old mind can't quite grasp the way the world works.

If I'm being honest, my twenty-nine-year-old mind can't always grasp the way the world works either.

What is clear to me is a mystery to my three-year-old. And what's clear to God is so often a mystery to me. How often I have to remind myself that what is confusing and frustrating to me is crystal clear to God. When I don't understand why or how things work, he does.

In the same way that I am patient with her insistence that one day I will return to a state of infancy, God is patient with me when I repeatedly insist that my ways are the best. Because he sees what I cannot.

Alisa

Praying God's Word When You Don't Understand His Ways

As the heavens are higher than the earth,
　　so are my ways higher than your ways
　　and my thoughts than your thoughts.
　　　(Isa. 55:9)

Abba Father, thank you that you see clearly when I don't. I don't always understand why this world is the way it is. I don't understand why things happen in this world. I don't understand why you—all-powerful and all-knowing—allow bad things to happen. But I know your ways and your thoughts are higher than mine.

We know and rely on the love God has for us. God is love. Whoever lives in love lives in God, and God in them. (1 John 4:16)

We know that in all things God works for the good of those who love him, who have been called according to his purpose. (Rom. 8:28)

Lord, even when I don't understand you, I can rely on you, because you are love. And because no one loves me like you, the Author of love, I can trust you with my life. Lord, you promised that all things work together for the good of those who love you. I love you, Lord. I trust you. And I want my life to be used for your purposes. Jesus, use me. Use me to further your kingdom.

> For God was pleased to have all his fullness dwell in him, and through him to reconcile to himself all things, whether things on earth or things in heaven, by making peace through his blood, shed on the cross. (Col. 1:19–20)

Christ Jesus, all fullness and richness and goodness in life dwell in you. Reconcile me to you. Forgive me for not trusting your love—for thinking that I know better or my ways are higher. They are not. Lord, even when I may not comprehend your ways, help me to never doubt the truth of the cross—that you have reconciled all things to yourself through the shedding of your blood.

Practical Steps

It's easy to make friends. If you count all 3,865 of my Facebook friends, along with the women in our church, the authors and speakers involved with my Speaker Chicks ministry, the people I meet at speaking events, and the friends at my literary agency, I'd say I have more than 5,000 "friends."

But the kinds of friends who know that the only green thing you've eaten in the last year is mint chocolate chip ice cream, and still cheer you on as you join the gym, are much, much harder to come by. When we're talking real, true, call-you-up-in-tears-at-two-in-the-morning friends, I have only six. And one of them is Roger.

When I contemplate the people in my life with whom I have deep, meaningful relationships, I realize that while they are all amazing and giving and genuine and God-fearing people, the true reason that our relationships go beyond the occasional wall post is because we've worked at our friendships. We've made an effort to get to know each other on a deeper level. I let them into my life. I gave them the chance to see past my floors covered with dog hair and the unfolded laundry piled onto the bed, and to see me for who I am.

God is the same way. He sees all the messes in your life. He sees your struggles, your weaknesses, those moments when you completely crack under the pressure. But he looks right past them and straight into your heart. Then he waits. He waits for you to turn to him and say, "Lord, I'm here. This is me. I want to know you." And then he moves right in.

So how do we welcome God into a deeper relationship with us? I think the best way is to seek him wholeheartedly. Here are four ways.

1. **Pray fervently.** It's easy to get caught up in formulaic praying: "Dear God, thanks for everything. Help me to have a good day. Amen." While I firmly believe that

anytime you pray, God is listening, I also feel like the more passionate and heartfelt your prayers are, the better you'll understand God and his ways. So when you pray, lay it all out there. Get real with God.

2. **Seek solitude.** I love people. (See: 3,865 Facebook friends.) There are days when I am surrounded by people from the moment I wake up until the moment I go to sleep. And that's a good thing—I have a whole army cheering me on, supporting me, making me laugh, loving me. But when I consider the times I've heard God's voice and felt his presence, I've always been alone. I urge you to seek solitude every day—get away from the kids, your husband, and your life and find somewhere quiet to just be. And listen.

3. **Read his Word.** My friend told me the other day that she has a hard time talking to God because he's not tangible. And she's right—he's not sitting here in my office with me as I write this, telling me his opinion, coaching me on which words to say and how to say them. But he did give us all a pretty good instruction manual. The Bible makes it pretty clear what God thinks about a lot of things, and I've found that the more I read and strive to understand his Word, the closer I feel to him.

4. **Get connected.** I can't imagine where my spiritual life would be if it weren't for Roger, my friends Debbie and Lanette, and my pastor, Scott Simmerok. They've prayed with me. They've studied the Word with me. They've held me accountable when I let my emotional

breakdown of 2011 draw me away from God instead of toward him. I firmly believe that community—whether it's through a church or a MOPS group or a small community group—is essential to building a close relationship with Christ.

6

Your Relationships
with Others

Though I know intellectually how vulnerable I
am to pride and power, I am the last one to know
when I succumb to their seduction. That's why
spiritual Lone Rangers are so dangerous—and
why we must depend on trusted brothers and sisters who love us enough to tell us the truth.

Chuck Colson

You're never going to find me escaping to a quiet cabin in
the woods to write. Not only because I hate bugs and cannot
stand to go even twenty-four hours without my Starbucks,
but also because I like to be around people.

Solitude is not my forte.

I'm a people person! I thrive on crowds. I love a good (Silpada) party. I'm at my best when I'm surrounded by laughter and noise and tons of women clamoring to get a look at my latest Target shoe department find.

And yet, with all my love for people, it used to be a rare occasion that I spent time praying for my friends.

Human relationships are important! They are among the only things that have eternal significance, and with that in mind, I want to support you as you <u>pray for your relationships to thrive</u>.

Praying God's Word for Your Friends

> Two are better than one,
>> because they have a good return for their
>> labor:
>> If either of them falls down,
>> one can help the other up.
> But pity anyone who falls
>> and has no one to help them up.
> Also, if two lie down together, they will keep
>> warm.
>> But how can one keep warm alone?
> Though one may be overpowered,
>> two can defend themselves.
> <u>A cord of three strands is not quickly broken</u>. (Eccles. 4:9–12)

O sovereign God, you say that two are better than one, and you're right. Only when I'm with others do I have the help I need to navigate the trials of this world. Thank you for providing me with friends—with people who love me in spite of my faults. Lord, make us a cord of many strands. Help us stand beside each other and give warmth when we're cold; help us lift each other up when we fall and defend each other in our daily battles.

The righteous choose their friends carefully,
    but the way of the wicked leads them
        astray. (Prov. 12:26)

Lord, give me wisdom to choose friends who will lead me toward you and not away from your will. Give me the foresight to know which relationships to pour my heart and soul into.

One who loves a pure heart and who speaks
        with grace
    will have the king for a friend. (Prov.
        22:11)

Jesus, I pray that you will help me to sprinkle my words with grace and love. May I have a pure and gracious heart so I can be the friend others need.

Therefore if you have any encouragement
from being united with Christ, if any comfort from his love, if any common sharing
in the Spirit, if any tenderness and compassion, then make my joy complete by being
like-minded, having the same love, being one
in spirit and of one mind. Do nothing out
of selfish ambition or vain conceit. Rather,

in humility value others above yourselves,
not looking to your own interests but each
of you to the interests of the others. (Phil.
2:1–4)

*Lord God, I want to honor you with my friendships.
Because you first loved me, I want to love as you love.
Give me tenderness and compassion in my relationships. I pray that you will help me to be unselfish when
it comes to others—help me to rely on you so I can love
others as you do.*

———————

Praise be to you, LORD,
    the God of our father Israel,
    from everlasting to everlasting.
Yours, LORD, is the greatness and the power
    and the glory and the majesty and the
        splendor,
    for everything in heaven and earth is
        yours. (1 Chron. 29:10–11)

*I praise you for giving me strong relationships that
help me to learn, grow, and thrive. I know you are my
Father and that all good things come from you. With
that in mind, I worship you in your greatness, majesty,
and splendor. Everything in heaven and earth is yours,
including my relationships. Take them and do with
them what you will.*

———————

When You're Struggling with Personal Conflict

Tracy was not someone I wanted to spend any more time with than I had to. Sadly, here I was again.

We both belonged to the same organization, and she was one of the leaders. She was good at what she did—one of the best—and she had no problem letting me know she was the expert and I had a lot to learn.

It was true—I did have a lot to learn. But when she gave me criticism and correction, she seemed to take a little too much pleasure in it. She would criticize the way I spoke, the clothes I wore, and the choices I made. She would do so in front of people—people I respected—and it always cut my heart.

And that's when I started to grow bitter.

I would say things about Tracy—I would talk about what a poor leader she was and how mean she was. Without fully realizing what I was doing, I was undermining Tracy at every event.

When I finally had a mirror held up to my behavior, I realized that the only way to really, truly change was for God to change my heart. I started to pray. But it seemed impossible. How do you get along with someone who is so set on not getting along with you?

I claimed Romans 12:18 as my verse to help in this relationship: "If it is possible, as far as it depends on you, live at peace with everyone." God wasn't saying I had to control Tracy's actions; I only had to control mine.

As I prayed, God gave me a new vision of who Tracy was. She was actually growing insecure because our group was changing so fast and she felt she couldn't keep up. The only way she could maintain control was to put others in their place. As soon as I saw that her jabs were not personal—that they came from her own insecurities—I was able to be much more at peace in the situation.

Yes, my stomach still does a little flip-flop when I see her, but now, after lots of prayer, I can be at peace.

Praying God's Word in the Midst of Conflict

How good and pleasant it is
when God's people live together in unity!
(Ps. 133:1)

God, it is good when my relationships are in unity. I know this. Yet at times, I struggle to avoid conflict. Please help me to live at peace with others.

What causes fights and quarrels among you? Don't they come from your desires that battle within you? You desire but do not have, so you kill. You covet but you cannot get what you want, so you quarrel and fight. You do not have because you do not ask God. When you ask, you do not receive, because you ask with wrong motives, that you may spend what you get on your pleasures. (James 4:1–3)

Lord, my quarrels may seem significant now, but truly they are nothing compared to your eternal purposes. I pray that you will reveal your heart to me so I can get along with others—even when it's difficult. Lord, give me a spirit that is others-seeking and forgiving.

Brothers and sisters, do not slander one another. Anyone who speaks against a brother or sister or judges them speaks against the law and judges it. When you judge the law, you are not keeping it, but sitting in judgment on it. There is only one Lawgiver and Judge, the one who is able to save and destroy. But you—who are you to judge your neighbor? (James 1:11–12)

Jesus, you are the ultimate judge. And yet I am tempted to slander other people. I judge them according to my standards instead of simply loving them and leaving the judgment to you. Lord, you are the lawgiver and judge, and I humbly give you my conflicts.

Humble yourselves before the Lord, and he will lift you up. (James 4:10)

Lord, I know I have played a role in the conflict I'm having right now. I ask your forgiveness. Give me the words to say so I can make peace with my friend. God, humble my heart.

7

Your Marriage

If you pray for yourself and not for your husband, you'll never find the blessings and fulfillment you want. What happens to him happens to you and you can't get around it.

Stormie Omartian

I don't have a great track record when it comes to marriage.

After my first marriage failed, I ended up alone, living with my parents at the tender age of thirty-four, and a single mom to my two kids. So, as you can imagine, I wasn't gung ho about jumping back onto the matrimonial bandwagon.

But then there was Roger—wonderful Roger—and our relationship was nothing like my former one. Roger was patient and kind and God-seeking and—get this—prayerful when it came to our relationship. He was not like any man I had ever met! And as much as I'd been hurt in the past, Roger won me over. I began to warm up to the idea of getting married again.

As Roger and I vowed to love and cherish each other forever, I also vowed to diligently pray for my marriage. I wasn't going to fail this time.

And I've been true to that vow. Those of you who have read my book *Praying God's Word for Your Husband* know I didn't always pray the right words or even with the right heart, but I've prayed for my marriage since day one. And it's made a world of difference.

Praying God's Word for Your Husband

His divine power has given us everything we need for a godly life through our knowledge of him who called us by his own glory and goodness. Through these he has given us his very great and precious promises, so that through them you may participate in the divine nature, having escaped the corruption in the world caused by evil desires. (2 Pet. 1:3–4)

Almighty God, you have given my husband everything he needs to live a life worthy of your calling. Thank you! I pray for my husband today. I pray that through your glory and goodness, your purposes for him will be revealed. I thank you for making such great and precious promises to us. Fill my husband with hope. May his heart sing your praises and his soul feel your glory as he goes about his day.

For this very reason, make every effort to
add to your faith goodness; and to goodness,
knowledge; and to knowledge, self-control;
and to self-control, perseverance; and to perseverance, godliness; and to godliness, mutual affection; and to mutual affection, love.
For if you possess these qualities in increasing measure, they will keep you from being
ineffective and unproductive in your knowledge of our Lord Jesus Christ. But whoever
does not have them is nearsighted and blind,
forgetting that they have been cleansed from
their past sins. (2 Pet. 1:5–9)

*Lord, you have blessed me with a wonderful man! I am
so grateful for my husband and the leader he is in our
family. I pray that you will bless him with continued
growth. Add goodness to his faith. Add knowledge to
his goodness. Add self-control to his knowledge. Add
perseverance to his self-control. Add godliness to his
perseverance. Add mutual affection to his godliness.
Add love to his mutual affection. Give him virtue in
increasing measure so he can be cleansed, renewed,
and invigorated.*

Be strong and courageous. Do not be afraid
or terrified because of them, for the LORD
your God goes with you; he will never leave
you nor forsake you. (Deut. 31:6)

*Lord Jesus, I pray that you will give my husband
strength and courage to persevere in the work before*

him today. Remind him that you are with him always and that you will never leave or forsake him.

For the grace of God has appeared that offers salvation to all people. It teaches us to say "No" to ungodliness and worldly passions, and to live self-controlled, upright and godly lives in this present age, while we wait for the blessed hope—the appearing of the glory of our great God and Savior, Jesus Christ, who gave himself for us to redeem us from all wickedness and to purify for himself a people that are his very own, eager to do what is good. (Titus 2:11–14)

Your grace is sufficient, O God! Fill my husband with your grace—the grace that assures him of salvation but also helps free him from temptations. Lord, reveal yourself to him today so he becomes the man you want him to be—a man who seeks you first and is eager to do what is good.

Therefore, my dear friends, as you have always obeyed—not only in my presence, but now much more in my absence—continue to work out your salvation with fear and trembling, for it is God who works in you to will and to act in order to fulfill his good purpose. (Phil. 2:12–13)

Intervene in my husband's life, Lord, so he will have no doubt of your presence in his life. Draw him close to you today, holding him tightly in your palm so he is protected physically, spiritually, and emotionally. Help him know that you are working out your perfect will in him.

Praying God's Word for Your Role as a Wife

This section is based on 1 Corinthians 13.

If I speak in the tongues of men or of angels, but do not have love, I am only a resounding gong or a clanging cymbal. If I have the gift of prophecy and can fathom all mysteries and all knowledge, and if I have a faith that can move mountains, but do not have love, I am nothing. If I give all I possess to the poor and give over my body to hardship that I may boast, but do not have love, I gain nothing. (vv. 1–3)

Jesus, I want to love my husband in a way that pleases you. Please help me to never let anything in this world turn me into a resounding gong! I realize that worldly pursuits—money, approval, and success—are nothing without love. So fill me with love that can come only from you—especially when it comes to loving my husband.

73

Love is patient, love is kind. It does not envy,
it does not boast, it is not proud. (v. 4)

*Father, I want to love my husband with this kind of
love! Give me patience, Lord. Teach me to be kind. Fill
my heart with a desire to treat my husband compassionately and empathetically. Help me to be quick to
forgive and slow to get angry.*

*Holy Father, take away any envious thoughts I have
toward my husband. You have blessed us with different skills and gifts, and I refuse to let those differences
stand in the way of my love.*

*Likewise, O Lord, keep boastful words from my
tongue. Everything I have is from you.*

[Love] does not dishonor others, it is not
self-seeking, it is not easily angered, it keeps
no record of wrongs. Love does not delight
in evil but rejoices with the truth. It always
protects, always trusts, always hopes, always
perseveres. (vv. 5–7)

*Lord, there are times I'm selfish—I seek my own gain by
dishonoring my husband or getting angry. But I know
you delight in the truth. Help me to reject evil and to
become a peacemaking wife who always protects my
husband's dignity, always trusts his words and actions,
always hopes for our future, and always perseveres,
even when times are tough.*

Love never fails. But where there are prophe-
cies, they will cease; where there are tongues,

they will be stilled; where there is knowledge, it will pass away. For we know in part and we prophesy in part, but when completeness comes, what is in part disappears. When I was a child, I talked like a child, I thought like a child, I reasoned like a child. When I became a man, I put the ways of childhood behind me. For now we see only a reflection as in a mirror; then we shall see face to face. Now I know in part; then I shall know fully, even as I am fully known. (vv. 8–12)

Precious Jesus, your love never fails. Ever! Everything in this world—even those things that seem the most tenacious and enduring—will pass away. But your love will never disappear. I can trust it always. And so can my husband. Lord, give my husband the faith of a man who understands your love. Help him to see your face and to know you as he is known.

And now these three remain: faith, hope and love. But the greatest of these is love. (v. 13)

Give me love for my husband, Lord. I want to honor him with a love that reflects yours. No matter what happens in this world, I know nothing will separate us from your love.

Praying God's Word When There Is Conflict in Your Marriage

A new command I give you: Love one another. As I have loved you, so you must love one another. By this everyone will know that you are my disciples, if you love one another. (John 13:34–35)

Lord Jesus, I want to love my husband in a Christlike way, just as you have commanded. I pray that you will help me to love him humbly, selflessly, compassionately, and kindly. Let your love shine through my actions.

———

The LORD God said, "It is not good for the man to be alone. I will make a helper suitable for him." (Gen. 2:18)

God, I was created as a helpmate for my husband. I am his other half. Raise me up as a helper for him—someone he can trust to come alongside him and support him in ways that honor you.

———

Do everything without grumbling or arguing, so that you may become blameless and pure, "children of God without fault in a warped and crooked generation." Then you will shine among them like stars in the sky as you hold firmly to the word of life. And then I will be able to boast on the day of Christ that I did not run or labor in vain. But even if I am being poured out like a drink offering

on the sacrifice and service coming from
your faith, I am glad and rejoice with all of
you. So you too should be glad and rejoice
with me. (Phil. 2:14–18)

*Jesus, I confess that I tend to grumble and argue with my
husband when things don't go my way. Please forgive
me! I want to be blameless and pure in your sight. Help
me to become a light that shines for my husband—
someone he can trust to take the high road when there
is conflict. Help me to joyfully and willingly pursue
peace, even when it's difficult.*

Make every effort to live in peace with
everyone and to be holy; without holiness no
one will see the Lord. See to it that no one
falls short of the grace of God and that no
bitter root grows up to cause trouble and de-
file many. (Heb. 12:14–15)

*God, when my husband and I fight, I grow bitter. I
need you to come into our relationship and purify it. I
know we both fall short of your glory, but I also know
you can sanctify and redeem any and every situation.
Give us the desire and the ability to live in peace with
each other.*

Therefore if you have any encouragement
from being united with Christ, if any comfort from his love, if any common sharing
in the Spirit, if any tenderness and compassion, then make my joy complete by being

like-minded, having the same love, being one in spirit and of one mind. Do nothing out of selfish ambition or vain conceit. Rather, in humility value others above yourselves, not looking to your own interests but each of you to the interests of the others. In your relationships with one another, have the same mindset as Christ Jesus. (Phil. 2:1–5)

Jesus, I know it is your will that my husband and I get along. You have joined us with you and have asked that we become one in spirit and mind. And you have promised us joy when we live in unity. Thank you! I humbly ask that you give our relationship an undying spirit of unity. Remove my selfish ambitions, Lord, so I can seek my husband's needs first in our marriage.

I want you to realize that the head of every man is Christ, and the head of the woman is man, and the head of Christ is God. (1 Cor. 11:3)

Submit to one another out of reverence for Christ. (Eph. 5:21)

Loving Father, you are in charge of our marriage. You have ordained us to become one flesh, one spirit, and one mind. When there is conflict, I want to turn to you first so I can treat my husband in a way that honors both him and you. Lord, please forgive me. Help me to show my husband how much I love him. Give me a willingness to bend my will out of reverence for you and love for my husband.

Practical Steps

What a blessing it is to your husband to be prayed for! Of course, God is working in his life through your prayers whether he knows it or not, but why not let him know you're talking to God about him behind the scenes? Here are six little ways to let him know you're remembering him in prayer.

1. **Post-it notes.** If any of you have read my book *The Husband Project*, you know I have an undeniable love for office supplies. So one thing I do is write little Post-its for Roger that tell him how great I think he is and tack them around the house—to his bathroom mirror, on his steering wheel, on his pillow. Next time you pray Scripture over your husband, try writing him a note: "Prayed God would make 2 Peter 1 real in your life today. XOXO!"

2. **Let him hear you pray.** No one ever said you had to actually be quiet during quiet time. So pray loudly enough for your husband to overhear as you pray Scripture over his life.

3. **Text him.** Send your husband a text message telling him that you've been praying for him, or just text him part of the prayer you've prayed.

4. **Pray with him.** Pull your husband aside and tell him you'd like to pray with him, then bless him by focusing the prayer time on him. (Hint: This is not one of those times that you should plead with God to help your husband learn to take out the garbage the first time you ask.)

5. **Serve Scripture with his breakfast.** Bring him breakfast in bed—or coffee, if you're feeling slammed—and hand him a Bible along with a list of the verses you've been praying for him.

6. **Leave a note.** Put a note in his lunch box—or his wallet, if he's one of those grown-ups who buys his lunch at a restaurant—and tell him the words you've been praying for him.

8

Parenthood

We know the excitement of getting a present—we love to unwrap it to see what is inside. So it is with our children—they are gifts we unwrap for years as we discover the unique characters God has made them.

Cornelius Plantinga Jr.

This might just be the easiest chapter in the whole book.

No, not because your kids are perfect and don't need prayer (ha!), but because as mothers, we all want what's best for our kids. And since as Christians, we know God has a perfect plan laid out for those who love him, it's a natural thing to start praying that God would carry out that plan in our children's lives.

I have prayed for my children diligently since day one of their lives. It was as if God spurred something in my soul that made me want to cry out to him for the sake of my precious babies. And even now that my kids are adults, their needs pop into my mind first every time I sit down to pray.

A few years ago, I decided to pray the book of Ephesians over my kids. I bought a brand-spanking-new prayer journal and wrote the opening verses in Ephesians at the top of the first page:

> Praise be to the God and Father of our Lord Jesus Christ, who has blessed us in the heavenly realms with every spiritual blessing in Christ. For he chose us in him before the creation of the world to be holy and blameless in his sight. In love he predestined us for adoption to sonship through Jesus Christ, in accordance with his pleasure and will—to the praise of his glorious grace, which he has freely given us in the One he loves. (Eph. 1:3–6)

And then I prayed that verse over my kids.

> *Praise you, Father, for blessing my kids with every spiritual blessing in Christ! Thank you that you chose them before the creation of the world to be holy and blameless in your sight.*
>
> *You have adopted my children—my Justen, my Kimberly, my Jeremy, my Amanda—as your own according to your amazing love. And you did it with pleasure!*
>
> *Jesus, I am so grateful that you have chosen my children as yours. You've given your grace freely to them*

*because you love them. Thank you, Jesus! All praise
and honor and glory are yours.*

Every day, I opened my Bible and my prayer journal and
prayed another couple of verses from Ephesians over my
kids' lives. It took almost eight months to finish praying the
book over my kids—eight months of reading and writing and
praying—but as I prayed, God revealed many truths to me.

- My kids—their bodies, their hearts, their goals, and their
  talents—belong to him, not to me.

- All praise and glory for the people they are and the things
  they do belong to him.

- God's salvation—free to all who love him—is the most
  glorious and wonderful gift that a mother could ask for
  her kids.

- Even when my kids are behaving in a way that doesn't
  honor Christ, his love for them is bigger, wider, deeper,
  and stronger than I know.

- I can face the world only with the belt of truth around
  my waist and the breastplate of righteousness across
  my chest.

All that said, I've written some specific prayers in this chapter to help you start praying Scripture for your children—but I
know that's not enough. So I encourage you to choose a book
in the Bible—I chose Ephesians, but Romans or Galatians
would be great too—and spend a few months praying the
entire book over your children's lives. I can assure you that
God will work powerfully through your prayers.

When You're Worried about Your Kids

I always thought I'd be a laid-back mom—one of the cool ones who doesn't stress about every little thing with her kids and knows when to back off because sometimes they have to learn on their own. Before kids, I operated under the "it'll all work out somehow" motto. But somewhere between cracking open the pregnancy books and delivering my firstborn, I went from my typical easygoing self to an overanalyzing, worst-case-scenario person I didn't even recognize.

I began living in the land of what-ifs and overthinking decisions because I felt so enormously responsible for the consequences. It started with things that directly affected my children and spilled over into life in general. A healthy dose of concern can be good at times, but fear was beginning to rule nearly all of my decisions.

My prayer life was practically nonexistent, and I felt the separation like when a good friend starts to become distant. I was irrationally terrified that admitting to the Lord that my family is really in his hands and not mine would somehow lead to terrible things happening as a test of my conviction, no matter how far-fetched I knew that was. Fear had laughed in the face of my common sense and deep-rooted beliefs. My human nature was falling for that sneaky little original lie that God doesn't know or want the best for our lives. How despicable that Satan took something as beautiful as becoming a mother to divide me from God.

But how incredible to me that the Lord rescues and restores beauty when we come to him facedown in tears, wholly surrendered. How amazing that my simple prayer of "Lord, they are yours and not mine" left me feeling not helpless but filled with relief and a desire to be closer to him than ever. It was the beginning of transformation.

It didn't happen overnight or with big, momentous changes. Instead, it was a slow chipping away at the wall of distrust I'd built between the Lord and me. Quiet surrender during Sunday morning worship. Prayers and discussions with girlfriends at Bible study. A season of Lent in which I decided to give up worry and replace it with prayer, fully realizing how often I battled the issue. Times of fear that left me nowhere to go but on my knees in prayer so emotional that at times I couldn't speak out loud. Glimpses of how much I so desperately need God and how he made it so perfectly to be that way. I realized how glorifying it is to him when I go to him in prayer and give it *all*—over and over again.

I still struggle at times, of course. But now when fear creeps in, I let prayer drown it out. I remember to "Be anxious for nothing, but in everything by prayer and supplication, with thanksgiving, let your requests be made known to God" (Phil. 4:6 NKJV).

Katie

Praying God's Word When You're Worried about Your Kids

> Be anxious for nothing, but in everything by prayer and supplication, with thanksgiving, let your requests be made known to God. (Phil. 4:6 NKJV)

Father God, you tell me to be anxious for nothing, but when it comes to my kids, I have a hard time. They are my most precious treasure—and when I start to think of them, my mama bear claws come out. I want them to be safe and happy and to know you, and I confess that I worry that something or somebody is going to hurt them or tear them away from following you. But you have asked me to make my requests known to you by prayer and supplication and with thanksgiving in my heart. So I'm going to do that.

The LORD will keep you from all harm—
    he will watch over your life;
the LORD will watch over your coming and
      going
    both now and forevermore. (Ps. 121:7–8)

Jesus, I pray for my children's safety and health. You have promised that you will watch over the lives of those who serve you. I pray that you will cover my children with your protection. Lord, protect them from illness and injury and keep their bodies healthy, vibrant, and strong.

Bring them up in the training and instruction
of the Lord. (Eph. 6:4)

More than anything, I want my children to know you, Lord. Help me to live my life in a way that my children see you and your glory in everything I do. Give me wise words to instruct them and patience to train them to be men and women of character.

The LORD is my strength and my shield;
    my heart trusts in him, and he helps me.

My heart leaps for joy,
and with my song I praise him. (Ps. 28:7)

*O God, I give my children to you. I hand my requests
to you with thanks that you are my children's strength
and shield. Help me to trust you deep in my heart with
my children. My heart is joyful that I can give them to
you, because you and you alone can protect and love
them with a wholly unselfish and perfect love.*

Seek first his kingdom and his righteousness,
and all these things will be given to you as
well. Therefore do not worry about tomorrow, for tomorrow will worry about itself.
Each day has enough trouble of its own.
(Matt. 6:33–34)

*Lord, when I start to worry about my kids—about their
health, their safety, their happiness, or their future—I
pray that I'll learn to turn to you first. Help me to seek
your righteousness so I can get help from the one who
knows what's best for my children. Take this worry
from my heart so I am able to enjoy my children and
this journey that you have taken me on.*

Teaching Your Kids to Pray

Sometimes I make sure my kids interrupt my prayer time.

On many mornings, I get up before anyone else does so I
can find some solitude and spend time alone with God. But
on some mornings, I purposefully pray when I know my

kids will catch me doing it—so they can see me praying and (hopefully) want to start to pray on their own.

So I head to the kitchen and bang around a little as I make my coffee. I slam the refrigerator door. Clank a few dishes on the counter. Stir my cream in loudly. Then I head back to the couch and open my Bible and my prayer journal.

My strategy rarely fails. A few minutes later, I'll hear the pitter-patter of little feet bounding down the stairs. Little tow-heads will peek into the living room and say, "Hi, Mommy! Whatcha doin'?"

"Praying. Want to join me?"

"Sure!" Slippered feet will skip over to the couch and snuggle in next to me. Little hands will reach for the note-book and pencil that I keep next to mine, and with precious words and pictures—straight from my kids' souls to God's ears—my kids will make their thoughts, feelings, and requests known to God.

Just this week, my sweet four-year-old daughter, Kate, joined me as I prayed for my nephew Asa. Asa was born with his intestines outside of his body and was having major surgery. We set up a prayer chain, and I signed up for the 6:30 a.m. spot. Kate asked to pray with me, so I handed her a notebook and pencil, and while I poured my heart out to God for my sweet nephew, she poured her innocent prayer onto lined paper.

"Dear Jesus, be with Asa and me and Joey and Will and Haddie. Keep Asa safe. Amen. Kate."

Simple words but powerful words, because God answers prayer. And when a child pours out her heart to the almighty Creator, God moves mountains.

My prayer is that my kids will never doubt that they can turn to God for anything and everything—whether it's a tiny anthill or a big mountain that needs moving.

Erin

Praying God's Word as Your Kids Learn to Pray

Jesus called the children to him and said, "Let the little children come to me, and do not hinder them, for the kingdom of God belongs to such as these." (Luke 18:16)

Heavenly Father, thank you for caring about my children. It's hard to imagine anyone could love them as much as I love them, but you do. You have given your entire kingdom to your precious children! So let my children come to you, Lord. Teach them to turn to you when they feel sad, happy, angry, lonely, scared, or joyful. Show them that they always have a friend in you no matter where they turn.

Come, my children, listen to me;
    I will teach you the fear of the LORD.
        (Ps. 34:11)

Dear brothers and sisters, pattern your lives after mine, and learn from those who follow our example. (Phil. 3:17 NLT)

I want to teach my children to live their lives in awe of you, Lord. Give me wisdom so that with every word I say and everything I do, my kids learn a little more about you. Help my actions to lead them to you. I pray that I will live in a way that demonstrates my love for you every day, every hour, every minute.

Be joyful in hope, patient in affliction, faithful in prayer. (Rom. 12:12)

Jesus, I want my children to be full of joy because of the hope they have in you. Your promises are my most treasured gifts, and I pray that you will fill my children with the joy of your promises as well. Help me to demonstrate patience so they will know the trials of this world are nothing compared to the glorious riches we have in you. I want to pray faithfully and courageously for your will in my life, and I ask that you make prayer a priority in each of my children's hearts as well. Help them to know they can turn to you for anything and everything they need.

Praying God's Word for Yourself as a Mother

Be shepherds of God's flock that is under your care, watching over them—not because you must, but because you are willing, as God wants you to be; not pursuing dishonest gain, but eager to serve. (1 Pet. 5:2)

God, you have entrusted me with these precious children. I thank you. I am humbly grateful for the opportunity to parent these precious souls and to teach them about you. Lord, I am willing to be the mother you intend me to be. I am willing to watch my children, to care for them, to serve them, to love them. Come beside me and help me to do this to the best of my ability.

Listen to my instruction and be wise;
    do not disregard it. (Prov. 8:33)

Sovereign Father, give me wisdom! I admit that I do not always know what to do or say. Help me to seek your wisdom to raise my children in a godly manner.

I pray that out of his glorious riches he may
strengthen you with power through his Spirit
in your inner being, so that Christ may dwell
in your hearts through faith. And I pray that
you, being rooted and established in love,
may have power, together with all the Lord's
holy people, to grasp how wide and long and
high and deep is the love of Christ, and to
know this love that surpasses knowledge—
that you may be filled to the measure of all
the fullness of God. (Eph. 3:16–19)

Lord, you have come to dwell in my heart. You have filled me with your glorious riches from the top of my head to the tips of my toes. I know you have given me everything I need to be the mother you created me to be. As I go about my day, give me the ability to grasp how wide and long and high and deep your love is. Help my cup to overflow with your love so I can pour it out on my children. Fill me with you today, God.

9

When You Feel Inadequate

The strength of a man consists in finding out the way in which God is going, and going in that way too.

Henry Ward Beecher

It was a dream opportunity.

I'd met a new friend (in my world, all we have to do is meet and you will have the title *friend*) who worked for a huge church. Huge. Like TV-show huge. After knowing me for a few months, she asked if I might be interested in speaking to a women's group at Gigantor Church. I immediately said yes. After all, I had a new book coming out, it seemed like a cool ministry, and I thought, *Why not?*

So I arrived at the church after a long flight and a longer drive. I ducked into the bathroom to change and get my makeup on. I was a little concerned that I would look okay. After all, I'm a laid-back California girl, and this gig was deep in the heart of Texas, where everyone was wearing heels and dressed to the hilt in Southern charm.

The one thing I didn't have to worry about was my hair. Let's just say that whether I'm in Texas or not, I have big hair. It's kinky and curly and over the top in a 1987 prom sort of way.

So I put on my jacket and my jewelry, fluffed my hair, and tried desperately to duplicate the makeup techniques that the twenty-year-old at the MAC counter taught me. I was good to go and actually pretty pleased with the results.

And then I saw my friend.

The first thing she asked me: "Do you want to go change?"

Ummm . . . into the yoga pants I wore on the plane? No, I'm good.

"Do you want some time to fix your hair and makeup?"

Ummm . . . since I'm the one who broke them, I guess not.

So my new friend decided she was going to give me a make-over—right then and there in the middle of the church. She called in a friend who was a stylist for some of the people on staff (yes, apparently that's a real job at this church), and they fluffed, primped, and made me over. Now I looked like a tired clown in a leopard jacket. That look? I was not pulling it off.

And then I realized why these girls were so nervous: they were introducing me to their boss.

This woman, after introducing herself, spent about ten minutes telling me all the places she had been and the ministry she had done.

And then, with about five minutes before I was to go onstage, she left me with these words: "Our leadership team is such a strong group that our ladies rarely enjoy outside speakers."

Awesome.

In that moment, I had a choice. My first option was to turn inward and wallow in a pity party of one. The second option was to pray. But I couldn't think of what to pray. (Have you ever had prayer panic? I was in the midst of it right there.) So instead, I started to think through one of my favorite verses, Isaiah 41:10 (NKJV):

> Fear not, for I am with you;
> Be not dismayed, for I am your God;
> I will strengthen you,
> Yes, I will help you,
> I will uphold you with My righteous right hand.

So that's what I started praying. I felt inadequate. I felt ugly. I felt small. But God was with me. It didn't matter what I was feeling; the fact was that God was upholding me.

I got up and spoke to those women. Afterward, God allowed me the privilege of seeing the results of his work through me: ladies lined up to let me know how much they needed to hear my words. I stood there praying for each of those women.

It is not my job to please an audience—most of the time I could do that under my own strength. My job is to do what God has called me to do, whatever the circumstances.

Praying God's Word When You Feel Inadequate

Let us then approach God's throne of grace with confidence, so that we may receive mercy and find grace to help us in our time of need. (Heb. 4:16)

O Father, I approach your throne with confidence because I know you are standing behind me and giving me the strength I need. Lord, I feel inadequate right now. I feel like there is no way I am capable of doing what's expected of me. I am not good enough, talented enough, holy enough, righteous enough, or faithful enough. But you are! You are more than enough for me. I pray that you will shower me with your mercy and grace.

What strength do I have, that I should still hope?
What prospects, that I should be patient?
Do I have the strength of stone?
Is my flesh bronze?
Do I have any power to help myself,
now that success has been driven from me? (Job 6:11–13)

Almighty God, on my own I have no strength to do the work you gave me. I feel insufficient, incapable. My body is weak and my mind is fragile, but you, O God, are my strength. Of my own accord, I do not have the power to succeed at anything. But you do.

I lift up my eyes to the mountains—
　　where does my help come from?
My help comes from the LORD,
　　the Maker of heaven and earth.
　　　　(Ps. 121:1–2)

O Maker of heaven and earth, you are my advocate. My help comes from you. When I'm feeling tiny and insignificant, incapable and inadequate, I pray that you will give me the foresight to turn my eyes to you, the one my help comes from.

He will not let your foot slip—
　　he who watches over you will not slumber;
indeed, he who watches over Israel
　　will neither slumber nor sleep.
The LORD watches over you—
　　the LORD is your shade at your right hand;
　　the sun will not harm you by day,
　　nor the moon by night.
The LORD will keep you from all harm—
　　he will watch over your life;
the LORD will watch over your coming and
　　　　going
　　both now and forevermore. (Ps. 121:3–8)

Lord, you stand beside me, strong and infallible when I'm at my weakest. You will not let me fall. What comfort I take in knowing that I serve a living God who is awake and always watching. Lord, my heart screams, "I can't do this!" but you take my hand and stand with me right now. And I can do this because you are watching over everything I do with your everlasting love and power.

Lord, be gracious to us;
    we long for you.
Be our strength every morning,
    our salvation in time of distress.
      (Isa. 33:2)

Lord, shower your grace on me. Come beside me; be my strength and salvation today and every day. I pray that you would free me from the distress of feeling inadequate or incapable. I know with you behind me, I am more than capable of doing the work you gave me.

You are my strength, I sing praise to you;
    you, God, are my fortress,
    my God on whom I can rely. (Ps. 59:17)

My fortress, you are my strength! I praise you with everything I am and everything I do, because I can rely on you to be my strength when I am weak, my voice when I have no words, my song when I am despairing, and my advocate when I feel inadequate.

When You Feel Inadequate about Your Appearance

You know those mornings when you somehow manage to get your kid out of their pajamas and ready for school, but you don't even have a second to look in the mirror before you hop in the car, so you show up at preschool drop-off with bed head while wearing your husband's old Mariners T-shirt? I've affectionately deemed that the "preschool walk of shame." And let's just say that I walk that walk nearly *every school morning.*

With all that in mind, you'd think that things like unwashed hair, sallow skin, and a teeny bit (okay, a lot-a-bit) of weight gain wouldn't even faze me. But awhile back, I had a full-on meltdown about my appearance.

It had been a really tough few months. I had gotten pregnant in May and found out eight weeks later that my tiny baby had health problems that were incompatible with life. I was devastated. And while we chose to keep the pregnancy as long as God allowed it, I admit that I soothed my soul with a lot of chocolate ice cream over the next few weeks. I lost that precious baby when I was fifteen weeks pregnant—a bittersweet time when God whispered to my soul in the midst of tragedy, comforting me with the fact that he had a perfect plan for each and every life on earth.

I had all these big, heartbreaking things going on in my life, and to top it all off (I know this sounds totally shallow in comparison), I had gained twenty pounds during my short pregnancy. And with the hair loss and skin changes that come from a lost pregnancy, I was feeling pretty unsightly.

Just as I was feeling my worst, emotionally *and* physically, I found out that I needed to take a work trip—a trip where

I'd meet people I had worked with for more than four years and had never once met. I completely melted down.

Tears streamed down my face as I explained to my husband that I just couldn't go—these people would never look at me the same way. And as many times as he reminded me that these people knew and respected me—they'd worked with me for years and weren't worried about what I looked like—I just couldn't get over my less-than-adequate appearance.

Finally, when my confidence was at my lowest, I turned to God. I prayed for a way out—a way to avoid or postpone the trip so my co-workers wouldn't see me in my "ugly phase." I prayed that he'd help me lose the weight quickly or restore my hair and skin to their pre-pregnancy glory. I prayed for confidence. I prayed that my appearance wouldn't be so consuming.

And God answered my prayer in a way that I never would've imagined. No, I didn't miraculously lose twenty pounds in a month. And no, the trip wasn't postponed or canceled. Instead, just three weeks after I lost my baby, I was absolutely shocked to find out that I was pregnant once again—this time with my precious (and healthy) son Will.

With that pregnancy in its early phases, I lost some of the weight, and my hair and skin changed yet again. And God showed me that while my appearance is insignificant in comparison to the larger plans he has for my life, he's willing and able to intervene on my behalf—in ways that are much bigger than I could ever imagine.

Erin

Praying God's Word When You Feel Inadequate about Your Appearance

Great is the LORD, and most worthy of
    praise,
  in the city of our God, his holy mountain.
Beautiful in its loftiness,
    the joy of the whole earth,
like the heights of Zaphon is Mount Zion,
    the city of the Great King.
God is in her citadels;
    he has shown himself to be her fortress.
      (Ps. 48:1–3)

Lord Jesus, you are beautiful. As I gaze upon your love-liness, I am amazed at how great, how powerful, and how worthy you truly are. Lord, I praise you for being my fortress and my strength.

First seek the counsel of the LORD.
(2 Chron. 18:4)

God, you ask me to seek your counsel first, and right now I am feeling like my appearance is inadequate. Lord, remind me that the way I look on the outside is insignificant compared to what is on the inside.

Charm is deceptive, and beauty is fleeting;
  but a woman who fears the LORD is to be
    praised. (Prov. 31:30)

O God, you tell me that true beauty comes from loving you with my entire heart, soul, and mind, yet there are times when my outward appearance matters to me— probably more than it should. Lord, help me to seek you and your kingdom first in everything I do so that the shallow things of this world, such as beauty, pale in comparison to your glory.

Give praise to the LORD, proclaim his name;
    make known among the nations what he
        has done.
Sing to him, sing praise to him;
    tell of all his wonderful acts.
Glory in his holy name;
    let the hearts of those who seek the LORD
        rejoice.
Look to the LORD and his strength;
    seek his face always. (1 Chron. 16:8–11)

Almighty God, replace the worries I have over my appearance with praise for you. Help me to sing your praises morning, noon, and night, telling the world who you are and about your holy name. I pray that I am able to seek your face and put aside the small and insignificant things that distract from your glory.

Practical Steps

My tendency when I feel inadequate is to withdraw into myself. I pull away, afraid that if I put myself out there, I'll fail.

But that's not the way God wants any of us to live—especially when we're feeling like we're not enough.

When Jesus sent his disciples out into the mission field, he told them:

> I am sending you out like sheep among wolves. Therefore be as shrewd as snakes and as innocent as doves. Be on your guard; you will be handed over to the local councils and be flogged in the synagogues. On my account you will be brought before governors and kings as witnesses to them and to the Gentiles. But when they arrest you, do not worry about what to say or how to say it. At that time you will be given what to say, for it will not be you speaking, but the Spirit of your Father speaking through you. (Matt. 10:16–20)

With those instructions in mind, here are some tips on how to respond when you're feeling insufficient to carry out the work God has given you.

1. **Be as shrewd as snakes.** I am a people pleaser. I'm nice. I like to be nice. I like helping people. But there are times when people just aren't going to be pleased—and no matter how much honey I drizzle on my words, they're just going to hear what they want to hear. In these times, I remind myself that even Jesus asked his disciples to be shrewd. This doesn't mean being unethical or rude or mean, but it does mean standing up for what's right even when it's unpopular.

2. **Be as innocent as doves.** Christ is my ultimate authority, and it's my responsibility to live up to his standards, no matter how much simpler it would be to conform to the world's.

3. **Be on your guard.** In the story I told earlier, it would've been really easy to get swept into the excitement and glamour of the stylists and cheering crowds and name-dropping that came with being at Gigantor Church. But instead, I felt unsettled. And when I reflect on that, I was unsettled because something was amiss—it seemed like the leaders weren't necessarily working to build *God's* kingdom but were working to build their own. By recognizing that, I was able to confidently step forward and speak from my heart without worrying about what they thought. I was worried only about what God thought.

4. **Do not worry about what to say or how to say it because God will speak through you.** Yep, it says right there in the Bible that God will give us the words to say. I know the Spirit of my Father is speaking and acting through me. What comfort! Although I may not be enough, he is!

10

When You're at Work

If God is satisfied with the work, the work may
be satisfied with itself.

C. S. Lewis

I was a newly single mom and I was desperate for a job.

Okay, I was 99 percent desperate. I really wanted and
needed a job, but I was also praying that God would allow
me one qualification: I prayed that whatever job he gave me
wouldn't require a hairnet. I had worked food services before—I didn't want to work that hard.

So I prayed and I prayed. And for three months, nothing
happened. Not one bite, not one returned phone call. Nothing. I was about to go get a hairnet as a sign of contrition,
and then it happened: I got not one but three job offers in

the space of a couple of days. And none of them required a hairnet.

One job was as an office worker, another as a sales rep, and the third as a radio salesperson. I told each company that I wanted the weekend to think about it, but it was obvious which one I was going to take: the radio salesperson.

I was single and in a new town. All the fun had been stripped out of my life. I wanted a job where I would look forward to getting up in the morning. I wanted a job where I could meet new people and have a great time, and the radio job was the perfect fit. I figured God owed me this since I was no longer going to be able to pursue the career I really wanted: writing, speaking, and planning women's events.

But before saying yes (because at some point I remembered I was a Christian), I figured I should pray about it and asked some of my friends to do the same.

Well, all my friends said the same thing: "I've been praying, and I think God is saying you're supposed to take the office job." I told them they needed to get a little more Jesus and pray again. But as the hours passed, it became more and more obvious: I was supposed to take the office job. And I did.

But let's be clear: I hated that job.

I hated the office work. I hated putting little numbers in little boxes all day long. Hated every minute of it.

Until one day the office manager asked if I would write a quick article for the update that went to all their supporters. So I did.

And then the president asked me if I would go to a speaking engagement for him and talk to a group of women. So I did.

And then the office started doing fund-raising and networking events—small pastors' breakfasts and large donor galas. So I worked on (and ran) some of those.

About three months into my job I realized, *I'm getting paid to speak, write, and plan events—everything I wanted to do before, but just in an entirely different way than I expected.*

I'm so glad that God doesn't give me what I want.

Praying God's Word for Your Work Life

By the grace of God I am what I am, and
his grace to me was not without effect. No,
I worked harder than all of them—yet not
I, but the grace of God that was with me.
(1 Cor. 15:10)

Father God, by your grace you have given me every talent and every skill that I have. I want to use these gifts for your glory. It is by your grace that I work and by your grace that I find success. I pray that I never forget that.

Jesus answered, "Very truly I tell you, you
are looking for me, not because you saw the
signs I performed but because you ate the
loaves and had your fill. Do not work for
food that spoils, but for food that endures to
eternal life, which the Son of Man will give
you. For on him God the Father has placed
his seal of approval." (John 6:26–27)

Lord God, I want everything I do on this earth to glorify you. As I go through each day, may my efforts go toward pleasing you and not toward accomplishing things that are of this world. I pray that you will guide me through each day so I can complete my tasks with your seal of approval.

Suppose one of you wants to build a tower. Won't you first sit down and estimate the cost to see if you have enough money to complete it? (Luke 14:28)

Jesus, give me wisdom as I work. I pray that you will give me a clear idea of the steps I need to take to have success. Help me to be wise in my business dealings.

Commit to the LORD whatever you do,
    and he will establish your plans.
        (Prov. 16:3)

Father God, I commit my career to you. I pray that you will guide me as I make decisions at work so I can do what's right by both you and my company. Thank you for helping me to succeed at work.

Whatever you do, work at it with all your heart, as working for the Lord, not for human masters, since you know that you will receive an inheritance from the Lord as a reward. It is the Lord Christ you are serving. (Col. 3:23–24)

All hard work brings a profit,
> but mere talk leads only to poverty.
>> (Prov. 14:23)

I pray that I can give my whole heart to the tasks that you lay before me at my job, Lord. I know that by serving my boss and my company in a giving, selfless, and courageous way, I am serving you. So give me the energy and tenacity to do my best today. I pray that you will make me a doer and not just a talker. I am judged at work by my actions and my productivity instead of by what I say, so I pray that by your grace I am able to accomplish the tasks I set out to complete.

Praying God's Word to Use Your Gifts and Talents for His Glory

This prayer is based on the parable of the talents in Matthew 25:14–30.

Loving Father, I want nothing more than to hear you say, "Well done, good and faithful servant!" As I work today, I pray that I will be like the man who had five bags of gold—wise, savvy, honest, trustworthy, and hardworking.

I pray for wisdom as I go through my work day. Help me to know how to use the talents and skills you have blessed me with to benefit my company and to honor you. When I have to make business decisions, I pray that I will consider all parties and all aspects of every decision so I know I am being fair and upright as I work.

Jesus, help me to multiply my talents in the workforce to the benefit of your kingdom. Even if my work tasks don't seem directly related to your kingdom, help me to do them in a way that makes people know without a doubt that I serve you, the living God.

At the end of today, O God, I want you to look at me and say, "Well done!" I pray that I am able to honor you with my work.

For Ethics at Work

I quit my dream job.

From 2005 to 2010, I had the job that made every single one of my friends jealous. I was working as a web writer and editor for a huge, famous company (did I mention they were big?) that most people would die to work for. I'm not even going to tell you the name of the company because you'd probably want to come over to my house right now and shake some sense into me for having the nerve to quit.

I made great money, worked part-time from home when my kids were napping, and had a byline on all sorts of newsletters and articles that went out to millions of subscribers. What's more—you're never going to believe this—since I wrote about pregnancy, babies, parenting, and food products and ideas, every day was like Christmas at my house. Companies would send me free products to review all the time. I'd come home from the gym and there would be a new $500 high chair on my porch. The next day, it was holiday clothes for my kids. The next, a stack of yet-to-be released cookbooks for me. I still have a huge stockpile of amazing free gear I got during the five years I worked that job.

And yes, I still quit.

And yes, there are days that I still wish I had that job.

But as I look back, quitting was the best decision I could've made. In spite of the tremendous perks, I was also working in an environment that was entirely focused on the wrong things. Where they wanted more money and more fame, I wanted to serve God and be a better mom.

For years, I ignored the ethics of my company and my boss so I wouldn't make waves at my dream job. I turned my head when people were treated unfairly. I pretended I didn't notice when people mocked God and mocked Christians. I smiled and worked harder when I noticed my company was doing things that I would consider less than ethical. And God convicted me.

In August 2010, I finally realized that enough was enough. And to the shock of everyone—including my boss and co-workers at that dream job—I quit. For months—no, years—I had people telling me things like, "I can't believe you left! You're crazy!"

But the truth is, I was crazy to stay there for so long. Now I realize that quitting was the best decision I ever made. I quickly got a new job as a writer and editor at another company—a company where I've never doubted the ethics or integrity of my boss or co-workers. And while my old job was full of glamour and glitz, my new job is steady. I look forward to working because I've never been asked to do anything that makes me feel uncomfortable. I've never been asked to lie, cheat, or nudge my ethics to the side in order to get ahead.

And that means something. Even if I don't get free gear in the mail anymore.

Erin

Praying God's Word for Your Ethics at Work

Every way of a man is right in his own eyes,
But the Lord weighs the hearts.
To do righteousness and justice
Is more acceptable to the Lord than sacri-
fice. (Prov. 21:2–3 NKJV)

Dear Jesus, I want to do what's right by you. Weigh my heart, O God. I pray that you will purify me so I can approach my work with pure motives and a righteous heart.

Blessed is the one
who does not walk in step with the
wicked
or stand in the way that sinners take
or sit in the company of mockers,
but whose delight is in the law of the Lord,
and who meditates on his law day and
night.
That person is like a tree planted by streams
of water,
which yields its fruit in season
and whose leaf does not wither—
whatever they do prospers. (Ps. 1:1–3)

Jesus, my work is important to me, but not so important that I'm willing to sacrifice my ethics or my faith for it. I pray that you will surround me with godly and trustworthy men and women so I can work at my job and work out my faith in you at the same time. But

Lord, I know there will be times that I work with people who don't know you. Help me to set an impeccable example of faith, love, and truth so they never question that I serve you. I pray that my faith and my career will prosper under your care and generous provision.

———

Because the Sovereign LORD helps me,
>   I will not be disgraced.
Therefore have I set my face like flint,
>   and I know I will not be put to shame.
He who vindicates me is near.
>   Who then will bring charges against me?
>   Let us face each other!
Who is my accuser?
>   Let him confront me!
It is the Sovereign LORD who helps me.
>   Who will condemn me?
They will all wear out like a garment;
>   the moths will eat them up. (Isa. 50:7–9)

Sovereign Lord, you are my helper. I know that in any and every situation, you are by my side and guiding me. Lord, give me the courage to face each day and each task knowing that you are my great helper. Guide me to deal with my business in a way that's honest, forthright, and true so no one can ever accuse me of wrongdoing or unethical behavior in the workplace.

———

The sleep of a laborer is sweet,
>   whether they eat little or much,
but as for the rich, their abundance
>   permits them no sleep. (Eccles. 5:12)

113

Jesus, help me to be a worker that you, my boss, and my company can be proud of. Sometimes I love my job and sometimes I struggle; give me the strength, energy, and tenacity to work hard and to work honestly. Give me peace and rest when I know I'm doing the right thing.

Practical Steps

Being a Christian in the workplace isn't easy, even for me—and I work for myself. Without a doubt, the best instruction manual about how we as Christians can live and thrive as workers is—you guessed it—the Bible.

I hang Post-it notes around my office with a few Proverbs that help me remember God as I work. If you're not as in love with office supplies as I am, you could put these verses on your laptop or keep a list in your wallet. For me, it's been really helpful to keep a constant, visual reminder of Christ with me as I work. Below are the Proverbs I have hanging around my office.

> **Proverbs 3:13 (ESV):** Blessed is the one who finds wisdom, and the one who gets understanding, for the gain from her is better than gain from silver and her profit better than gold.

> **Proverbs 10:4 (ESV):** A slack hand causes poverty, but the hand of the diligent makes rich.

> **Proverbs 11:1 (NASB):** A false balance is an abomination to the Lord, but a just weight is his delight.

Proverbs 16:1 (NASB): The plans of the heart belong to man, but the answer of the tongue is from the Lord.

Proverbs 18:15 (ESV): An intelligent heart acquires knowledge, and the ear of the wise seeks knowledge.

Proverbs 19:20 (ESV): Listen to advice and accept instruction, that you may gain wisdom in the future.

Proverbs 21:2 (NKJV): Every way of a man is right in his own eyes, but the Lord weighs the hearts.

Proverbs 21:3 (NKJV): To do righteousness and justice is more acceptable to the Lord than sacrifice.

Proverbs 21:25 (ESV): The plans of the diligent lead surely to abundance, but everyone who is hasty comes only to poverty.

11

Your Finances

Pray like it all depends on God, but work like it
all depends on you.

Dave Ramsey

I really wish I could be completely indifferent about money.

Wouldn't it be nice to just set the whole idea of money aside?
Never need it, never worry about it, never even *think* about it?

Let's face it: money is kind of important. In fact, it's pretty
much essential when it comes to things like paying the mortgage
and eating. And since as a general rule I enjoy sleeping with a
roof over my head and eating, money is a priority in my life.

Finding balance between God and money is one of the most
difficult things I do. I'm a freelance writer and speaker—which
means that Roger and I don't have a dependable monthly

income. There are times when the money flows in and I don't have to worry about how to pay the mortgage or the grocery bill. And I admit that at those times, my life feels simpler. Less stressful.

But there are other times when speaking gigs fall through or books aren't selling as well as I'd like them to, and we find we're struggling to make ends meet. My life starts to feel frantic and out of balance. Roger and I fight more. I am less generous with my time and resources. I start to get desperate. And I stop trusting God to provide.

It's frustrating that money plays such a role in my life and my emotions. I doubt that I'm the only one who is affected like this. Which is why I wrote this chapter—because if you're anything like me, finances are a hot-button issue in your life.

And there's no better way to handle a big issue than to let go and let God.

Praying God's Word for Wisdom with Your Finances

I keep asking that the God of our Lord Jesus Christ, the glorious Father, may give you the Spirit of wisdom and revelation, so that you may know him better. I pray that the eyes of your heart may be enlightened in order that you may know the hope to which he has called you, the riches of his glorious inheritance in his holy people. (Eph. 1:17–18)

Lord Jesus, you are my inheritance. The hope I have in you is all I need to live a rich and fulfilling life. I pray that you will give me wisdom as I make financial choices so whatever I do honors you. Show me your heart, Lord, so I can know you deeply and understand your will as I make financial decisions.

The wise store up choice food and olive oil,
    but fools gulp theirs down. (Prov. 21:20)

I want to be wise with my money. Please stop me from making foolish decisions, Lord, even when I stubbornly think I know best. Guide me, Lord. Give me your wisdom as I deal with my finances.

But godliness with contentment is great gain. For we brought nothing into the world, and we can take nothing out of it. But if we have food and clothing, we will be content with that. Those who want to get rich fall into temptation and a trap and into many foolish and harmful desires that plunge people into ruin and destruction. For the love of money is a root of all kinds of evil. Some people, eager for money, have wandered from the faith and pierced themselves with many griefs. (1 Tim. 6:6–10)

Keep your lives free from the love of money and be content with what you have, because God has said,
    "Never will I leave you;
        never will I forsake you." (Heb. 13:5)

Father God, help me to be content with what I have. You have given me so much, but I often fall into the temptation to want more, more, more. But more things will do nothing for me except pull me farther away from you. My true riches come from you, God. You will never leave me alone. You will never turn your back on me. And that is worth more than billions of dollars. Change the desires of my heart, Lord! Help me to desire you and you alone. I pray that my contentment comes from knowing you and not from anything else.

Whoever can be trusted with very little can also be trusted with much, and whoever is dishonest with very little will also be dishonest with much. So if you have not been trustworthy in handling worldly wealth, who will trust you with true riches? And if you have not been trustworthy with someone else's property, who will give you property of your own?

No one can serve two masters. Either you will hate the one and love the other, or you will be devoted to the one and despise the other. You cannot serve both God and money. (Luke 16:10–13)

O Lord, you have trusted me with your true riches! You have shared your hope and your wisdom and your love with me. And I want to serve you every day of my life as an act of worship to you. Lord, take away my love of money. Help me to work hard, to work honestly, and most important, to work for your gain instead of my own. I pray that you will find me trustworthy in all I do.

But where can wisdom be found?
  Where does understanding dwell?
No mortal comprehends its worth;
    it cannot be found in the land of the
      living.
The deep says, "It is not in me";
    the sea says, "It is not with me."
It cannot be bought with the finest gold,
    nor can its price be weighed out in silver.
It cannot be bought with the gold of Ophir,
    with precious onyx or lapis lazuli.
Neither gold nor crystal can compare with
      it,
    nor can it be had for jewels of gold.
Coral and jasper are not worthy of mention;
    the price of wisdom is beyond rubies.
The topaz of Cush cannot compare with it;
    it cannot be bought with pure gold.
Where then does wisdom come from?
  Where does understanding dwell?
    (Job 28:12–20)

O Father God, I know wisdom comes from you. I cannot make wise decisions in my life without your guidance. Take away my pride, Lord, so I can humbly search for answers from the one who knows all. Help me not to seek wisdom from human sources—from my own knowledge, from worldly pursuits, or from those who aren't seeking you—but instead, to seek your wisdom first.

When You Struggle with Finances

Why is prayer always a last resort?

I believe in prayer. I teach about prayer. But for some reason, when I'm in the midst of an issue, prayer becomes my "well, I've tried everything else" option. I blame this attitude on my own "bad girl" complex. I say to myself, "You got yourself into this, now you need to get yourself out," instead of "God will find a way."

This has been especially true when I've made bad decisions in my life in two big areas: money and men.

Thankfully, the men decisions (or should I say the *man* decisions) have improved radically in the past ten years since I met and married Roger. But finances are something that I still have issues with, especially as a freelance author. There have been more than a few times when either circumstances or, more likely, my bad planning have gotten me into trouble.

We've all heard of the five stages of grief. But here is my very own list—the "Five Stages of Financial Grief and the Freaking Out That Follows."

1. *Panic.* "Oh no! There isn't enough money left at the end of the month. What are we going to do? How will we pay the bills? How will we afford groceries?"

2. *Blame.* "We wouldn't be in this mess if . . . [Roger paid more attention to the finances/my parents had taught me how to budget/my events paid me on time/the dog hadn't gotten sick]."

3. *Justify.* "If only . . . [the cat hadn't had that weird bump/ the economy wasn't in a free fall/the bank hadn't put a

hold on that check], we would have been fine! It's not my fault."

4. *Scheme.* "Okay, in order to get out of this mess, I can . . . [sell something on eBay/borrow money from our household account for the business/lay off an employee/call everyone who owes me money and lean on them]."

5. *Pray.* The last resort.

This happened a couple of years ago when Roger and I were faced with an unexpectedly high tax bill. I went through all the phases. (Roger, being a bit farther down the road in his Christian walk, skipped a couple of the steps.) I was in a full-blown panic. I was immobilized and not thinking clearly. And when I'm in a panic, I tend to turn on those around me—and Roger was right there for the picking. I took my anxiety out on him. Poor guy!

And then, after all of the panicking, blaming, justifying, and scheming (not to mention the yelling, screaming, and ranting), I finally got to the end of myself and joined Roger in praying. I was embarrassed that it took me so long to get to what should have been my first choice.

After praying on our evening walk, Roger received an email from work reminding him about an account he had been paying into. Roger had set this account up years before we were married, and while he knew it was there, he didn't know it was something we had access to in order to get us over this financial hump. We were able to pay off the tax bill and pay the account back.

Some people would call it lucky that Roger received that email when he did. We know it was something else—when we finally decided to ask God for help, he answered our prayers in a direct and tangible way.

Praying God's Word When You're Struggling with Finances

Every good and perfect gift is from above, coming down from the Father of the heavenly lights, who does not change like shifting shadows. He chose to give us birth through the word of truth, that we might be a kind of firstfruits of all he created. (James 1:17–18)

Father of the heavenly lights, you never change! You are the same whether I am rich or poor, faithful or unfaithful, wise or unwise. God, while my financial situation is bleak right now, I know you understand and are watching over me. You have given me the very best of your creation—eternal life through the gift of your Son. Although I am poor in worldly possessions right now, I am rich in my life with you.

Whoever loves money never has enough;
   whoever loves wealth is never satisfied
      with their income.
   This too is meaningless.
As goods increase,
   so do those who consume them.
And what benefit are they to the owners
   except to feast their eyes on them?
The sleep of a laborer is sweet,
   whether they eat little or much,
but as for the rich, their abundance
   permits them no sleep. (Eccles. 5:10–12)

Lord, I know I need money to survive, but help me to see it for what it is and not allow it to consume me. I want to work to honor you, not to get more things. As I struggle with my finances right now, I want to make decisions that honor you, regardless of how they help my financial situation.

Rejoice in the Lord always. I will say it again: Rejoice! Let your gentleness be evident to all. The Lord is near. Do not be anxious about anything, but in every situation, by prayer and petition, with thanksgiving, present your requests to God. And the peace of God, which transcends all understanding, will guard your hearts and your minds in Christ Jesus. (Phil. 4:4–7)

I am joyful, Lord, not because I have worldly riches but because I have you. Your peace fills me with hope. I pray that you will remove my anxiety over finances, God. Help me to pray with a thankful and trusting heart. I know you will provide exactly what I need.

My God will meet all your needs according to the riches of his glory in Christ Jesus. (Phil. 4:19)

God, you promised to meet all of my needs, not because I deserve it but because of your wonderful grace. I trust that you will meet my needs right now, today. Perhaps you will do so in unexpected ways or in your timing instead of mine, but I know you will work miraculously in my life. And I am comforted.

Generosity

A few months ago, I was driving to a speaking event when I heard a pastor on the radio say, "It's really easy to see what a person values when you look at their bank account and see where their money is being spent."

Gulp.

Roger and I have always made giving to our church and to God a priority—we know how important it is to be generous with our finances. But if someone were to look at our bank account, they'd probably see that Starbucks and the Target shoe section rank as high priorities as well.

Don't get me wrong. There is nothing wrong with indulging in a nonfat vanilla latte with whip every once in a while. But God does ask us to be purposeful and intentional with how we spend our money. That often means sacrificing by giving generously both out of our excess and out of our want.

So I want to ask you to prayerfully consider how you can give generously out of what God has given you, so if someone looked at your bank account, they would see that God—his kingdom, his mission, his plans, his people, and his purposes—are your number one priority. Even if that means missing out on those super cute flats you just spotted at Target.

Praying God's Word
for a Generous Spirit

In everything I did, I showed you that by this kind of hard work we must help the weak, remembering the words the Lord Jesus himself said: "It is more blessed to give than to receive." (Acts 20:35)

126

Holy God, you have been so generous with me. You have given me everything, including your own Son! I pray that I am able to adopt your heart and be willing to give generously of everything I have.

One person gives freely, yet gains even more;
　　another withholds unduly, but comes to
　　　poverty.
A generous person will prosper;
　　whoever refreshes others will be refreshed.
　　　(Prov. 11:24–25)

God, my natural instinct is to cling to my worldly possessions, as if by holding tightly to what you have given me, I'll somehow gain more. But the truth is that you have called us to give freely and out of a generous spirit. So help me to let go—to have a loose fist on my money and my possessions. Give me a heart that willingly shares with those in need.

Do not store up for yourselves treasures on earth, where moths and vermin destroy, and where thieves break in and steal. But store up for yourselves treasures in heaven, where moths and vermin do not destroy, and where thieves do not break in and steal. For where your treasure is, there your heart will be also. (Matt. 6:19–21)

There is not a possession in this world that is worth anything! Every single thing I own is temporary, insignificant. Help me to store up treasures in heaven that show I'm living my life for you and your purposes.

Command those who are rich in this present world not to be arrogant nor to put their hope in wealth, which is so uncertain, but to put their hope in God, who richly provides us with everything for our enjoyment. Command them to do good, to be rich in good deeds, and to be generous and willing to share. In this way they will lay up treasure for themselves as a firm foundation for the coming age, so that they may take hold of the life that is truly life. (1 Tim. 6:17–19)

My hope comes from you, Lord, and not from my own riches, my own success, or my own works. I want to share the treasures you have given me with those who are lost or in need. You have richly provided me with so much, and I pray that I am willing to share these blessings—both the physical and the spiritual—with anyone and everyone. Help me to live in a way that's truly living out your perfect will for my life and my resources.

Give, and it will be given to you. A good measure, pressed down, shaken together and running over, will be poured into your lap. For with the measure you use, it will be measured to you. (Luke 6:38)

Lord, I give all I have to you! It's hard for me to generously offer all of my worldly treasures up to you as an offering of gratitude, but I am willing to because I love you. Lord, help me choose how to use what you have entrusted me with.

12

When You're Worried

Worry does not empty tomorrow of its sorrow;
it empties today of its strength.

Corrie ten Boom

I'm a selective worrier. I don't worry about earthquakes (even
though I live near San Francisco) or anything else that is
completely out of my control. What I do worry about are
those things that I have the illusion of having some control
over: my kids, my marriage, my work, my finances.

I'm like a dog gnawing on a bone. I work that worry bone
over and over until my gums are raw. I worry that I haven't
done enough or that my kids will do what they want to do,
not what I want them to do. I worry that our money will run
out or my work will run out. I worry that I will look like a

fool. The more I worry, the more immobilized I am. I stay stuck where I am, working over that bone.

I usually spend a couple of days in a worry pit, not talking to God about my fears. (I always feel like, "I've made this mess, now I need to get out of it.") And then I become that living cautionary tale of what Corrie ten Boom said: I lose my strength in the moment.

As I spend more time studying and understanding the nature of God, I know the ultimate act of distrust toward him is my most natural reaction—worry. And the only antidote that is at all effective against that worry is prayer and reading God's Word.

As I get older, it gets easier not to go for days before turning to God. Yes, sometimes I still take hours, but there is no reason to live for days, or weeks on end, worrying.

When You're Worried
(about Your Kids, Your Family, Your Job, Your Finances, Anything)

When my best friend learned she was pregnant with her first child, we were elated together. This was a much-prayed-for baby, and we gave thanks. So it did not make sense when we learned at the twenty-week sonogram that Katie's sweet little girl would not survive birth. Emotions tumbled from a high point of happiness to deep grief.

The next few months were hard, a time of mourning even as Katie and her husband embraced every movement, every captured heartbeat of their daughter. They loved her completely. This child was worth it. In between the love, we all cried together. I already had two little boys, and my mother-heart could not grasp the pain.

One particular night, we had a great Central Texas storm that kept me awake for hours. I felt so nauseous too. Because I could not sleep, I prayed. I felt someone was hurting, and I prayed for comfort. In between prayers, I hugged the toilet. Why was I so sick?

Finally, later that morning, I took a pregnancy test. Sure enough, our third child was on the way. After the first thrill, I choked. What would I tell Katie? I picked up my phone, trying to decide what to do. It was early, so I was surprised by a text message from Katie. That night during the storm, her daughter had been born and had gone to be with the Lord.

Tears streamed down my face. Why this morning? And why pray? Why pray for my own child if my prayers have no sway in the heavenly realm? If I believe God works everything for good and is sovereign, what place do my requests have? I felt guilty praying for my child. Still, my heart longed to pray for the baby's health. I was so torn.

"Stop it," my husband said as he pulled me into a hug. "We pray because God told us to pray, and that's it." (See James 5:13–18.)

That calmed me down for the moment, but it was Katie, in all her own hurt and struggle, who helped me the most. She reminded me of what happened in Gethsemane and Jesus's own prayer in Mark 14:32–40. Jesus described what he felt as "overwhelmed with sorrow to the point of death."

The passage continues, "Going a little farther, he fell to the ground and prayed that if possible the hour might pass from him. 'Abba, Father,' he said, 'everything is possible for you. Take this cup from me. Yet not what I will, but what you will.'"

First, Jesus in all his humanity prayed that death would not come. Then he submitted to a higher calling because he trusted God's plan. So maybe it's okay to lift up the prayer of my heart. Maybe I pray it not because God needs to hear it but because I need to say it. And when I meet with him, I remember he conquered death.

So dear Abba, I pray for my child, for this baby's health, and for this little one to be able to say, "Yet not what I will, but what you will." Amen.

Christi

Praying God's Word
When You're Worried

I have told you all this so that you may have peace in me. Here on earth you will have many trials and sorrows. But take heart, because I have overcome the world. (John 16:33 NLT)

Father, why do I worry? Yes, I have trials. Yes, I have sorrows. But you have overcome the world! How wonderful to know that you, the God of the universe, are in control of everything. And even more, you care about me on a personal level. Lord, fill me with your peace— the peace that comes from knowing that you in your infinite power and wisdom are in control of my life.

Jesus said, "That is why I tell you not to worry about everyday life—whether you have enough food to eat or enough clothes to wear. For life is more than food, and your body more than clothing. Look at the ravens. They don't plant or harvest or store food in barns, for God feeds them. And you are far more valuable to him than any birds! Can all your worries add a single moment to your life? And if worry can't accomplish a little thing like that, what's the use of worrying over bigger things?" (Luke 12:22–26 NLT)

Lord, you make it clear there is no reason to worry about the small things in life—money, trivial work issues, tiny offenses—yet for some reason, I find myself overcome. These things gnaw at me. I wonder how I'm going to pay the bills. I wonder how to stretch my time. Yet those things are not worth worrying about. Help me to spend my time thinking about bigger and better things—things that have eternal significance. Lord, erase these worries from my mind and fill my thoughts with you instead.

Commit everything you do to the LORD.
    Trust him, and he will help you.
He will make your innocence radiate like the
        dawn,
    and the justice of your cause will shine
        like the noonday sun. (Ps. 37:5–6 NLT)

Lord, you ask me to commit everything I do to you, and I want to do exactly that. I trust you with my life—with my relationships, with my finances, with my health, with everything I do and everything I am. I take such comfort in knowing that you will help me. You are my advocate in a dark world. You are the light I need to traverse this life.

He said to me, "My grace is sufficient for you, for my power is made perfect in weakness." Therefore I will boast all the more gladly about my weaknesses, so that Christ's power may rest on me. (2 Cor. 12:9)

My gracious Father, I spend so much time worrying about how I can fix things that I forget that your power is made perfect in my weakness. You are so powerful, and you will do your good work in spite of me. It's amazing to think that you, my God and Creator, are working out the intricate details of my life for good. Thank you, Jesus!

Cast all your anxiety on him because he cares for you. (1 Pet. 5:7)

Abba Father, you care about me! And not just about the big picture of my life, but about every single tiny detail. Thank you, Jesus, for caring for me. Lord, I give you my worries, the big ones and the small ones. I give you everything. Please take this burden from me.

I lift up my eyes to the mountains—
     where does my help come from?
My help comes from the LORD,
     the Maker of heaven and earth.
          (Ps. 121:1–2)

Christ Jesus, I turn to you. Thank you for being my helper and my deliverer. I am in awe of your kindness and your grace. I hand my worries over to you right now. Fill my heart with your peace—peace that comes from knowing that the Author of life and Creator of

*the universe is quietly orchestrating my life. There is
no reason to worry.*

Now to him who is able to do immeasurably
more than all we ask or imagine, according to
his power that is at work within us. (Eph. 3:20)

*Father God, you are able to do immeasurably more than
I can even imagine. Today I will trust that your power
is at work within me. Fill me with your presence so I
can step forward confidently, knowing that you have
already taken care of everything for me. Amaze me
with your love, your power, and your grace in my life.*

Practical Steps

There is no magic cure-all for worrying. Even though I know
and believe that God is in control of my life, I still worry. A
lot. It's ridiculous, really, that I continue to fret even with the
Author of life in charge, but I do. And I'm guessing you do too.

But we are not hopeless. We are children of an all-powerful
Savior who wants us to cast our cares upon him. And with
that in mind, here are a few tricks that have helped me to calm
my anxious spirit when I start to be consumed with worry.

1. **Make a worry journal.** Buy a journal and use it to jot
   down all the things you're worried about. Every time
   you close the journal, remind yourself that the things
   you wrote down are God's and not yours.

2. **Have a worry prayer time.** Set aside five minutes each day to spend praying specifically for the things you worry about. Ask God to ease your mind and remind you that he is in control. When you say amen, take a deep breath and move on to thinking about other things.

3. **Be mindful of your worrying.** I sometimes catch myself hopping on the worry train and staying aboard for hours before I realize that I've wasted a lot of time heading in the wrong direction. Be cognizant of the times you start to spiral into worry, and when you do, immediately nip it in the bud by stopping to pray, calling a friend, or reading Scriptures.

4. **Meditate on God's promises.** God has given us so much, and sometimes all it takes to ease my worries is spending some time reading God's Word and thinking about him. Spend twenty minutes contemplating how big God's love is, how powerful his promises are, and how great the hope is that we have in him. Reading Psalm 92 is a great place to start.

5. **Be a servant.** One of the best ways to erase your own worries is to put your time, energy, and thoughts into helping someone else. The next time you're feeling overcome with worry, whip up a batch of cookies for a friend or offer to mow your neighbor's yard.

6. **Share your struggles.** Lean on the people God has put in your life. Call a friend to share your worries and ask her to pray with you, or ask your husband to spend some time talking about what's going through your mind.

13

When You're Despairing

Great hopes make great men.
Thomas Fuller

Have you ever faced a dark time in your life? A time when God seemed distant or unreal, when life seemed overwhelming, when difficult events or tough decisions left you depressed and despairing?

Sometimes a cloud of anguish can come upon you suddenly—you lose someone or something you love, a dream is smashed, your confidence is shaken. Or perhaps the darkness slowly seeps into your life—a wisp of depression that blooms into sorrow before you even know what has happened.

When I moved to Sacramento, I honestly thought my life was over.

Yes, I had two great kids, but because I was moving to get out of my marriage, I had two kids who were in a lot of pain.

I lost my house. My marriage was over. I went from being a homeschooling mom to a single mom working full-time at a job I hated. Oh, and for the ultimate indignity, I was now living with my parents.

This was not how I expected my life to turn out.

I had given up on hoping that life could get any better. I really did think, *This is my life now. I will never love anyone again, and God is punishing me and my kids for my mistakes.*

But as I started to pray, I began to feel a new version of normal. I was not alone in my despair! I had a heavenly Father who understood my suffering. He knew the feeling of despair. And before long, things in my life started to change, just slightly:

- The job I hated turned into one that I loved, with loads of co-workers who loved me and were praying for me.
- My mom made her home a soft place to land for this newly single mom and her kiddos.
- God truly became my husband during that time.
- God used that time to bring healing into my life.

Because of that time in my life, I am confident that I can turn to God on my darkest days and he will lead me into the light.

When You Feel Broken

We bought an older home last year. There are lots of projects that need attention. So many, in fact, that we mostly ignore them until something actually breaks.

Unbroken things don't require fixing. They just get used again and again and again, and no one thinks twice about them. The refrigerator that keeps the food cold is completely taken for granted. The garage door that the children haven't broken by repeatedly throwing a ball at it barely registers in my mind. The door that opens and closes easily without incident never draws me away from important matters like updating my status on Facebook.

But right now, there are a lot of broken things in this house. The ice maker leaks; the front door handle gets stuck; the garage door has panels missing; and the people around here lack patience, argue sometimes, and can be awfully stubborn.

Broken things get all the attention, all the prayer, all the time and money and focus.

In theory, we could bulldoze this old house and start over with a new one. No more thirty-six-year-old walls and electrical wires and plumbing. But even if we had the money to do that, I don't think we would. This place is our home, and we love it. As much as I would like to fix what is broken, I want even more to preserve what is lovely and unique about our home.

Sometimes, when I stare at the brokenness inside us all, I wonder why God doesn't just fix us. Couldn't he just snap his fingers and make everything that's wrong miraculously right?

I guess he could. But since he doesn't, he must want something from us and for us other than instant perfection. I am beginning to think he likes us with our flaws, temper tantrums, vanities, and lack of wisdom. Maybe, just maybe, perfection isn't his goal this side of heaven.

The truth is, I don't pray for my children when they are content and easy to understand. I don't pray for God's presence in our home very much when life sparkles with joy and we're all happy. I take my marriage for granted when there is no conflict or selfishness threatening to splinter our hearts.

I am ashamed to admit it, but if God snapped his fingers and fixed us all, he might never hear from me again.

So today, instead of begging for deliverance, I am going to praise him when my son looks me in the eye and refuses to share. I will gratefully take the hand of my tired and fussy little girl who is so mad she has fire shooting out of her ears. I will look in the mirror and smile at the selfish woman looking back at me and tell her to set her heart once more on obeying God.

I will face all of our brokenness, and my heart will sing an old song: "This is the day the LORD has made. We will rejoice and be glad in it" (Ps. 118:24 NLT).

As for the house, I think I need to find a good handyman. . . .

Carrie

Praying God's Word When You Feel Broken

> The righteous cry out, and the LORD hears
>   them;
>   he delivers them from all their troubles.
> The LORD is close to the brokenhearted
>   and saves those who are crushed in spirit.
>   (Ps. 34:17–18)

Father God, I cry out to you today, and you hear me. You deliver me from all my troubles—not just some, but all. You are my God; you are with me in this time of pain and sorrow. Deliver me, loving Father, in expected and unexpected ways, and restore me to wholeness.

You adulterous people, don't you know
that friendship with the world means en-
mity against God? Therefore, anyone who
chooses to be a friend of the world becomes
an enemy of God. Or do you think Scripture says without reason that he jealously
longs for the spirit he has caused to dwell in
us? But he gives us more grace. That is why
Scripture says:

"God opposes the proud
    but shows favor to the humble."
        (James 4:4–6)

*O God, rescue me from those things that do nothing
but pull me away from you. Instead, give me the grace
to innately understand you and your purpose for my
life. Give me more grace, and fill me with humility,
Lord, for I am nothing without you.*

Blessed are the poor in spirit,
    for theirs is the kingdom of heaven.
Blessed are those who mourn,
    for they will be comforted.
Blessed are the meek,
    for they will inherit the earth.
Blessed are those who hunger and thirst for
        righteousness,
    for they will be filled.
Blessed are the merciful,
    for they will be shown mercy.
Blessed are the pure in heart,
    for they will see God.

141

Blessed are the peacemakers,
  for they will be called children of God.
Blessed are those who are persecuted because
    of righteousness,
  for theirs is the kingdom of heaven.
    (Matt. 5:3–10)

Lord Jesus, you rain your blessings on those who are poor in spirit; who are meek; who have tears streaming down their faces as they hunger for righteousness; who are the merciful, the peace-seeking, and the persecuted. I pray for those who love you with the love of the brokenhearted. None of these qualities signify success in this world. None are symbols of power or wealth or prestige. Instead, all are characteristics of the humble— of people who recognize that brokenness is the only way to truly find God. I pray that my brokenness will lead me to the kingdom of heaven and that my tears will lead to unshakable faith, mercy, hope, and love.

Is anyone among you in trouble? Let them pray. Is anyone happy? Let them sing songs of praise. Is anyone among you sick? Let them call the elders of the church to pray over them and anoint them with oil in the name of the Lord. And the prayer offered in faith will make the sick person well; the Lord will raise them up. If they have sinned, they will be forgiven. Therefore confess your sins to each other and pray for each other so that you may be healed. The prayer of a righteous person is powerful and effective. (James 5:13–16)

Heal me, O Lord. Dry my tears and mend my broken heart. I come to you humbly in prayer, confessing that I have walked down the wrong path more often than not. I know I have struggled, I have sinned, and I have been proud. I come to you asking for forgiveness so I can be healed and restored into communion with you.

Praise be to the LORD,
    for he showed me the wonders of his love
    when I was in a city under siege.
In my alarm I said,
    "I am cut off from your sight!"
Yet you heard my cry for mercy
    when I called to you for help.
Love the LORD, all his faithful people!
The LORD preserves those who are true to him,
    but the proud he pays back in full.
Be strong and take heart,
    all you who hope in the LORD.
        (Ps. 31:21–24)

I am encouraged by your promises today, Lord. Even though my spirit is crushed, you have promised that you will preserve me. Your love is amazing—so wonderful that I cannot comprehend it. Your mercy is unequivocal—no one else can comfort me the way you can. Your hope is what restores me, because I know you have orchestrated everything for my good. I humbly thank you.

When you cry out for help,
    let your collection of idols save you!

The wind will carry all of them off,
    a mere breath will blow them away.
But whoever takes refuge in me
    will inherit the land
    and possess my holy mountain.
        (Isa. 57:13)

God, you are my refuge. I have cried out to you, the living God, and I know mere words from you can carry my troubles away. Thank you for a safe place to rest, and for being the friend I can rely on no matter what happens, no matter when, and no matter what I've done.

When You're Despairing

Sitting on my oversized living room couch, my already cooling coffee in hand, I reread the proverb for the thirteenth time.

"Hope deferred makes the heart sick,
    but a longing fulfilled is a tree of life."
    (Prov. 13:12)

I rolled it around on my tongue, contemplating and letting the words sink in. And then it dawned on me: there before me was my diagnosis. After almost two years of battling through infertility and adoption loss, I was left with a deep ache. My heart was sick. And the pain, which could only momentarily be forgotten while shopping at the outlet mall, be soothed with some good chocolate, or be lessened with a good cry, was always there, binding me to sorrow. No matter how hard I tried, the ache never really went away. But this morning, for the first time in months, something had actually touched the ache.

While the proverb offered little help in how my desires to expand our family could be fulfilled, the diagnosis of my heart soothed me. I saw clearly in words written thousands of years ago that long before my pain had begun, God truly understood my heart. He understood long before I was born that this season of deferred hope would leave me heartsick.

The words to the proverb can't bring me a child—my heart's desire—but they did address my pain. My all-powerful God knows that today my heart hurts.

Alisa

Praying God's Word When You're Despairing

For this is what the LORD says:
"I will extend peace to her like a river,
 and the wealth of nations like a flooding
 stream;
you will nurse and be carried on her arm
 and dandled on her knees.
As a mother comforts her child,
 so will I comfort you;
 and you will be comforted over Jerusalem." (Isa. 66:12–13)

Father God, you have promised me comfort even in my darkest days. Today I'm wallowing in darkness. I feel alone, as if I'm carrying these burdens on my own. Come beside me, O God, and extend your peace to me like a river. Be my comfort; hold me close. Help me to overflow with your peace.

Therefore we do not lose heart. Though out-
wardly we are wasting away, yet inwardly we
are being renewed day by day. For our light
and momentary troubles are achieving for
us an eternal glory that far outweighs them
all. So we fix our eyes not on what is seen,
but on what is unseen, since what is seen
is temporary, but what is unseen is eternal.
(2 Cor. 4:16–18)

*Abba Father, I cry out to you! I feel as if I'm wasting
away, slowly disintegrating into a pit of hopelessness.
But you have assured me that my spirit is being renewed
day by day. Reassure me that these troubles I'm facing,
although very real, are insignificant in comparison to
the eternal glory and hope I have in you. Give me eyes
only for you, God. Help me to push these temporary
struggles out of my mind and open my eyes to what's
eternal.*

Restore to me the joy of your salvation
    and grant me a willing spirit, to sustain
        me. (Ps. 51:12)

*Great Comforter, you see how I'm struggling. You see
my hopes and dreams. You see that I am feeling crushed
under the burdens of my life. Restore joy to me, Lord.
Grant me a spirit of willingness to put one foot in
front of the other and keep moving forward. Sustain
me with your peace, O God, so I will be filled with
hope instead of despair.*

Hope deferred makes the heart sick,
  but a longing fulfilled is a tree of life.
    (Prov. 13:12)

God, as I wait and long for my heart's desires to be fulfilled, help me to take comfort in knowing that you see. O Jesus, my heart is sick. I long for change. I long to be filled with your mercies again. Come beside me right now when my hopes seem distant and fill me with your peace.

Praise be to the God and Father of our Lord
Jesus Christ, the Father of compassion and
the God of all comfort, who comforts us
in all our troubles, so that we can comfort
those in any trouble with the comfort we
ourselves receive from God. For just as we
share abundantly in the sufferings of Christ,
so also our comfort abounds through Christ.
(2 Cor. 1:3–5)

Loving Father, I praise you. I praise you first and foremost for your Son, my Lord Jesus Christ, and for the joy of your salvation. I also praise you for your compassion, for being my comfort in my troubles, and for being my hope in darkness. Take from me this cup. Fill me with your joy so that I may comfort others with the abundance you have given me.

Practical Steps

Prayer is powerful. I think by this point in the book we can all agree on that. I firmly believe that God heals through prayer—and he can take you even from the pit of despair and restore you to joy simply because you ask him to. And I believe that there are some simple steps we can take in conjunction with prayer to keep us from being in that place of feeling despondent.

1. **Be in community.** Isolation is one of the surest ways to feel depressed. If you find yourself making excuses for not hanging out with friends or attending the Bible study you used to love, ask a friend to hold you accountable for getting together with others.

2. **Eat right.** When I'm leaning toward isolation and depression, the first thing to go is my willingness to prepare healthy meals. Take the time to nurture your body.

3. **Exercise.** Endorphins (the body's natural mood enhancers) are produced when you exercise. Make sure you are making time to move your body every single day—even if it's just walking your dog.

That being said, I don't want to minimize the effects of serious depression on Christian women around the country.

I've talked to countless women who feel that the idea of seeking help for depression shows weakness or that they aren't trusting God. There is nothing further from the truth! Depression is a very real and very serious illness—one that causes millions of women to suffer.

I've copied a list of questions below—adapted from a depression-symptom checklist on WebMD (www.webmd.com)—that will help you to determine if the despair you're feeling is a normal dip in your emotional life, or if it's something more. If you answer yes to one or more of the questions below, I want to encourage you to seek professional help (as I did) from a doctor or counselor. Whether or not you are suffering from depression, it is worthwhile to seek out someone who can help you to understand what you are going through and offer treatment if needed.

- Do you feel down, depressed, or hopeless most of the day?
- Have you lost interest in doing the things that you used to enjoy?
- Are you overly anxious?
- Are you excessively irritable?
- Are you sleeping more or less than you used to?
- Are you having trouble concentrating?
- Are you unable to effectively make decisions?
- Do you feel worthless?
- Do you feel guilty over things that you shouldn't feel guilty about?
- Are you fatigued for no apparent reason?
- Do you have unexplained headaches, stomach pain, or muscle pain?

14

Your Past Mistakes

The law works fear and wrath; grace works hope
and mercy.

Martin Luther

I will never forget where I was when my son called me out.

Roger, my kids, and I were in the parking lot of Oakridge Mall when Justen announced, "I know you were pregnant with me before you and Dad got married. Remember, I'm good at math."

Gulp.

It's not that I hid the information from Justen, I just figured that as a preteen boy, he hadn't really been paying attention to the date that his dad and I got married. And yes, if you did the math, you would realize that Justen was born about six months after our wedding.

Even though my life was totally different now—new husband, new ministry, new commitment to God and the way he wanted me to live—facts were facts. My past mistakes were following me, and the result from one mistake was my very loved young man who was great at math.

When You've Made a Mistake That Feels Unforgivable

Prayer is something that has been *present* throughout my entire life, but it hasn't exactly been *prevalent*. When I was a kid, prayer was my norm. The words that poured from my lips night after night were spoken to my heavenly Father. My prayers were those of thankfulness for the day, of pleading for children's lives that were coming to a close on the bone marrow transplant floor of Texas Children's Hospital, and of asking for his protection as I slept. That's what I remember. And then, somewhere along the line, the nightly supplications became a meaningless routine that declined more and more until they ultimately ended altogether, as though nighttime prayer was a childish thing I had done away with.

Don't get me wrong. I still prayed, but only after I had exhausted every other option. If I'm being honest, prayer was my last resort. It was the thing I turned to when I was at the very edge of a cliff and sometimes had already slipped, and while clinging white-knuckled to that overhanging rock, I would gasp out a desperate cry of a prayer. The problem was that I didn't pray with a right heart. Even when God responded mercifully by bringing me out of the pit, I would soon slip right back in. And the slips began to come closer and closer together. Living for the flesh became easy. It felt natural and good, and I soon stopped fighting against it.

The pleasures of this world are fleeting (see 1 John 2:17). How true! And how sadly ignorant I was to that fact.

At first I felt guilty for stepping onto the slippery slope of sin, but as I buried that feeling and continued to step-slip, there came a day when my guilt was just a vague memory. Nothing more. Like a day from years ago, it had become another part of my past. So I kept sliding. And then it happened. I slid too far too fast, and I was faced with a choice. The only thing that could save my reputation was an abortion. At least, that's what I told myself.

For a week I tried to talk my heart into it. I told myself, "It will be better this way. No one else will have to be affected by this. No one will be disappointed. I won't have to change my plans for myself. I won't have to give up anything. This will *ruin* my life." Those last words were spoken right from my guilt-seared conscience, and with raging ferocity, they pierced the deepest part of my heartstrings. I stopped. I couldn't fix this. Not by myself.

Like a child running in terror, eyes wide, scanning the surrounding faces for her father, I ran. Tears pouring, feet clambering, gasping in desperation, I ran to my Father. And the best part? He ran to me. With an embrace like I've never felt before in my life.

"God, Father," my heart screamed, "what do I *do*? I'm so sorry I didn't listen. I—I'm sorry . . ." The rest of that prayer? It was silence. I rested in his peace, listened to him, and my heart knew. The being forming inside of my body was a life. And my life? Well, it wasn't mine. "For none of us lives to himself, and none of us dies to himself. For if we live, we live to the Lord, and if we die, we die to the Lord. So then, whether we live or whether we die, we are the Lord's. For to this end Christ died and lived again" (Rom. 14:7–9 ESV).

I was still his. That hadn't changed. Through all the sin, the running, the ignoring, and now the shame, I had never stopped being his daughter. My future wasn't mine. My future now included that of a child's. *My* child's. What that future looked like, I had no idea. I just knew that my child would have one.

And because of this, I see the storms as the good and necessary times of my life—God is bringing me back to my knees, back to brokenness, and ultimately back to him.

Barbara

Praying God's Word When You've Done Something That Feels Unforgivable

In him we have redemption through his blood, the forgiveness of sins, in accordance with the riches of God's grace that he lavished on us. With all wisdom and understanding, he made known to us the mystery of his will according to his good pleasure, which he purposed in Christ, to be put into effect when the times reach their fulfillment—to bring unity to all things in heaven and on earth under Christ. (Eph. 1:7–10)

God, only you are holy and blameless. But through you and because of your amazing grace, I have redemption. I am so unworthy! While I deserve for you to turn away from me because of the things I have done, instead, you have lavished me with grace. I thank you, Lord, for continuing to stand by me and for showering your understanding and wisdom on me even when I don't deserve it.

The LORD did not set his affection on you and choose you because you were more numerous than other peoples, for you were the fewest of all peoples. But it was because the LORD loved you and kept the oath he swore to your ancestors that he brought you out with a mighty hand and redeemed you from the land of slavery, from the power of Pharaoh king of Egypt. (Deut. 7:7–8)

Father God, I know you did not choose me because of who I am. I am not wise enough or godly enough or holy enough to be chosen by you. But you chose me because you loved me. You redeemed me because of your great mercy. And I live in hope because you have brought me out of slavery and into your promises.

This is the message we have heard from him and declare to you: God is light; in him there is no darkness at all. If we claim to have fellowship with him and yet walk in the darkness, we lie and do not live out the truth. But if we walk in the light, as he is in the light, we have fellowship with one another, and the blood of Jesus, his Son, purifies us from all sin. (1 John 1:5–7)

Jesus, I have spent too much time walking in the darkness. I have deceived myself into thinking that what feels good is right. I humbly ask for forgiveness. I pray that you will draw me back to your light, Lord God, so I can once again walk in fellowship with you. Clean me, scrub out the dirt and grime in my life, and bring me back to innocence before you.

When tempted, no one should say, "God is tempting me." For God cannot be tempted by evil, nor does he tempt anyone; but each person is tempted when they are dragged away by their own evil desire and enticed. Then, after desire has conceived, it gives birth to sin; and sin, when it is full-grown, gives birth to death.

Don't be deceived, my dear brothers and sisters. Every good and perfect gift is from above, coming down from the Father of the heavenly lights, who does not change like shifting shadows. He chose to give us birth through the word of truth, that we might be a kind of first fruits of all he created. (James 1:13–18)

Lord, I have allowed temptation to direct me toward sin. And you've made it very clear that sin deserves death. Thank you for not giving up on me. Your love never wavers, even when I deserve to be separated from you. Forgive me and restore me. Thank you for filling my life with good and perfect gifts—the biggest and best being your salvation.

"All things have been committed to me by my Father. No one knows who the Son is except the Father, and no one knows who the Father is except the Son and those to whom the Son chooses to reveal him."

Then he turned to his disciples and said privately, "Blessed are the eyes that see what you see. For I tell you that many prophets and kings wanted to see what you see but did not see it, and to hear what you hear but did not hear it." (Luke 10:22–24)

Lord Jesus, you said that you will bless those who see you for who you are—the almighty Creator and God. I want to see you! Give me ears to hear your Word and a heart to seek your truth. Thank you for coming to offer forgiveness and redemption. Come beside me, Lord. I confess that I have fallen, and now I turn wholeheartedly to you with eyes wide open. Speak to me, Lord. I am ready to listen.

Praying God's Word for Forgiveness

Like a muddied spring or a polluted well
    are the righteous who give way to the
      wicked. (Prov. 25:26)

Jesus, I have become like a mud puddle—I've allowed dirt and grime to flow into my life, and now nothing is clean. I pray that you will restore me to righteousness.

If we claim to be without sin, we deceive
ourselves and the truth is not in us. If we
confess our sins, he is faithful and just and
will forgive us our sins and purify us from
all unrighteousness. If we claim we have not
sinned, we make him out to be a liar and his
word is not in us. (1 John 1:8–10)

*I've really messed up, God. I know my actions and my
thoughts haven't honored you in the slightest. But Lord,
when my relationship with you is broken by my sin,
nothing is right with me. I feel so lost and alone. Please
forgive me, Lord. Restore our relationship. You're all I
need to feel whole again.*

Catch for us the foxes,
   the little foxes
that ruin the vineyards,
   our vineyards that are in bloom.
    (Song of Sol. 2:15)

*Jesus, there are many little "foxes" in my life—things
that seem insignificant at first glance but then sweep
in and destroy everything good in my life. Catch those
foxes for me. Please stop them before they cause me to
stumble or walk away from you.*

If you love me, keep my commands.
    (John 14:15)

Because I do love you, Lord, I want to keep your commands. I know I am incapable of doing so on my own. Jesus, come beside me and help me to do what's right, even when it's hard.

Praying God's Word When You're Overcome by Guilt

Therefore, there is now no condemnation for those who are in Christ Jesus, because through Christ Jesus the law of the Spirit who gives life has set you free from the law of sin and death. For what the law was powerless to do because it was weakened by the flesh, God did by sending his own Son in the likeness of sinful flesh to be a sin offering. And so he condemned sin in the flesh, in order that the righteous requirement of the law might be fully met in us, who do not live according to the flesh but according to the Spirit. (Rom. 8:1–4)

Christ Jesus, please remove my guilt. You say there is no condemnation for those who are in you, and I am so grateful for that because I feel overcome by guilt right now. But you have set me free! Although I have sinned and I certainly don't deserve grace, you came for me so my shame would disappear. I thank you for your forgiveness, and I pray that your Spirit would flow into my life so I can let go of this guilt and move forward. I want to live a life that is redeemed!

For all have sinned and fall short of the glory of God, and all are justified freely by his grace through the redemption that came by Christ Jesus. (Rom. 3:23–24)

I have fallen short—way short—of your glory, Lord. I am heartbroken, but you have freely given me redemption through your grace. Jesus, fill my soul with that promise so I can move forward from this guilt, knowing that while I am completely undeserving, you have given me grace that surpasses all understanding. That grace—and your Son Jesus's incredible sacrifice—is all I need to remove this guilt from my life.

Jesus told them this parable: "Suppose one of you has a hundred sheep and loses one of them. Doesn't he leave the ninety-nine in the open country and go after the lost sheep until he finds it? And when he finds it, he joyfully puts it on his shoulders and goes home. Then he calls his friends and neighbors together and says, 'Rejoice with me; I have found my lost sheep.' I tell you that in the same way there will be more rejoicing in heaven over one sinner who repents than over ninety-nine righteous persons who do not need to repent." (Luke 15:3–7)

Father God, I am like that lost sheep—I have wandered from your fold over and over again. There are times I wonder why you haven't just let me go, allowing me to wander to my own destruction. Yet you don't work like that. You search me out, find me as I choose the wrong path, take me back into your loving arms, and restore me to safety. Jesus, hold me close and never let me go! I choose the abundant and joyful life that comes only from living in your arms. I thank you for always coming to find me. I want to be found!

My dear children, I write this to you so that you will not sin. But if anybody does sin, we have an advocate with the Father—Jesus Christ, the Righteous One. He is the atoning sacrifice for our sins, and not only for ours but also for the sins of the whole world. (1 John 2:1–2)

God made him who had no sin to be sin for us, so that in him we might become the righteousness of God. (2 Cor. 5:21)

O Righteous One, I am guilty, but you have removed that guilt. I find it hard to wrap my mind around the fact that you, Jesus—the one who lived a perfect and holy life—gave yourself as a sacrifice for me. Yet you did. And because of that sacrifice, I can live without carrying a heavy burden of guilt.

Praying God's Word to Honor Him with Your Body

For you created my inmost being;
    you knit me together in my mother's
        womb.

I praise you because I am fearfully and won-
derfully made;
your works are wonderful,
I know that full well.
My frame was not hidden from you
when I was made in the secret place,
when I was woven together in the depths
of the earth.
Your eyes saw my unformed body;
all the days ordained for me were written
in your book
before one of them came to be.
How precious to me are your thoughts, God!
How vast is the sum of them!
Were I to count them,
they would outnumber the grains of
sand—
when I awake, I am still with you.
(Ps. 139:13–18)

*O Great Creator, you are the one who made me the
person I am. Your Word says you knit me together in
my mother's womb, and that creates such a comforting
picture in my mind. You know every part of me—the
good and the bad, the beautiful and the ugly. Not a
single part of my physical body, my mind, or my soul
was a mistake. You chose to make me exactly as I am.*

Do you not know that your bodies are
temples of the Holy Spirit, who is in you,
whom you have received from God? You are
not your own; you were bought at a price.

Therefore honor God with your bodies.
(1 Cor. 6:19–20)

If anyone destroys God's temple, God will
destroy that person; for God's temple is
sacred, and you together are that temple.
(1 Cor. 3:17)

*Father God, when you say that my body is your temple,
I am convicted to take the utmost care of myself. I
know you designed me for a purpose, and I pray that
you will help me to use my body, mind, and soul for
that purpose. My body is sacred and has been set aside
for your work. Lord, give me the courage to honor you
with my body.*

Therefore, I urge you, brothers and sisters, in
view of God's mercy, to offer your bodies as
a living sacrifice, holy and pleasing to God—
this is your true and proper worship. Do not
conform to the pattern of this world, but be
transformed by the renewing of your mind.
Then you will be able to test and approve
what God's will is—his good, pleasing and
perfect will. (Rom. 12:1–2)

*Jesus, I am willing to give you everything I am. I offer
myself as a living sacrifice to worship you. Help me not
to be conformed to the pattern of this world. Transform
me as I renew my mind and meditate on your Word.
Use me as you will. O God, help me to shine as an
example of someone who takes every breath for you.*

Practical Steps

There is nothing you can do that will separate you from God's love.

Let me just say that again so you can let it sink in a little. There is absolutely *nothing* you can do that will separate you from the perfect, holy, and merciful love of God.

Isn't that comforting?

We've all slid down the slippery slope of sin—every one of us. We've done things that we're not proud of. We've felt unforgivable. We've allowed the things of this world to come before the things of God. And while that's human nature, God's nature is to come beside the repentant with grace and love and restore them to full communication with him.

So what do you do when you find yourself miles down a road that you should never have started on? How do you turn around, turn toward God, and get back on the right path? And even if you've already moved onto the right path, how do you get rid of the guilt of falling in the first place? Here are a few tips to get you started.

1. **Cry out to God.** It's so easy to get caught up in sin! And when I find myself in that place, my first instinct is to fight my way out of it—to start trudging back to God on my own. But that never works. Instead, I must turn to God. I must cry out to him in repentance, confess my mistake, and ask him for forgiveness. He will forgive me. Right then and there.

2. **Ask God for help.** It may be easy to get caught up in sin, but it's so hard to get out of it on your own. So

ask God for help—because even when the things you've done or are doing are too big for you, they're never too big for God.

3. **Find friends who can relate.** For years, I felt guilty about my out-of-wedlock pregnancy. I felt like I would be a church pariah for the rest of my life if anyone knew. But as I started to seek forgiveness and restoration, I found out that there are lots of women—lots of strong, godly women—who have dealt with the same issue. One such friend helped me to seek forgiveness. She also helped me to see that while I had made a mistake, God could use that mistake to make me stronger and even to influence other women for him as they learned about my forgiveness and restoration. He can do the same for you.

4. **Seek professional help.** If you're really struggling—either to escape sin or to escape the guilt from past sin—there's no shame in seeking guidance and help from a pastor or counselor.

5. **Give yourself grace.** I think it's often easier to forgive others than to forgive yourself. So give yourself some grace and be willing to move forward from past mistakes and focus on the future.

15

Your Health

A good laugh and a long sleep are the best cures
in the doctor's book.

Irish proverb

I hate being sick.

Okay, so everyone hates being sick. I'm not alone there.
But I have some extra loathing for illness right now because
in the recent past, I have battled with illness after sinus infec-
tion after illness. And I'm getting really tired of it.

You can trust me when I tell you that I'm not quiet about
my loathing. I cried when I lost my voice less than two hours
before a huge speaking conference that had been on my books
for a year. And when I was holed up with whooping cough, I
literally shouted at Roger (in a very hoarse sort of shouting

voice) about how miserable I was every single time he was within range (i.e., in the house).

But as much as I ranted and raved and loaded up on extra-strength Tylenol, I found myself shying away from prayer. It wasn't that I didn't believe God could heal me—I know for a fact that God heals in miraculous ways. (Just wait until you hear the story about my mom's healing from cancer later in this chapter.) But I worried that my little illnesses were insignificant in comparison to the things other people were facing.

Here's the thing: God is omnipotent. That means he's all-powerful and can manage to listen to your requests, big and small. And that means if you unload on him because you have a tiny splinter in your pinkie, he's listening. And he cares. So in this chapter, I'm going to guide you through how to pray for health—both yours and your loved ones'—whether you're asking for healing from a cold or from cancer.

When You're Not Healthy

Losing your voice is annoying anytime. But when you're teaching at a retreat, it's downright career limiting.

I knew it was going to be a hard retreat. I was feeling under the weather, losing my voice, and just downright miserable. And then an email came through from one of the pastors at the large church I was doing the retreat for. The devastating news was in front of me: the senior pastor and his wife had received the news that their adult son had died.

The leadership was reeling. I knew that when we got to the retreat center, most of the women would not know the news. I was at a loss on how to teach that weekend, and honestly, I was so sick I really couldn't think clearly. That's when I knew I needed prayer—and lots of it.

I sent an email to the GIMs (Girlfriends In Ministry). GIMs is a group of local women who are pastors, women's ministry directors, small group directors, and other leaders in the church.

Now, due to the nature of my ministry, I'm traveling a lot. In fact, from September to May, I don't unpack my suitcase—I just wash and reload. With doing that much travel, it's impossible to be part of a weekly Bible study. I would end up missing at least half of the meetings. So it's great that I have my GIMs. These are the women I know are praying for me, and I have the privilege of praying for them. Even if I can't make it to the monthly meeting, I know I can call on them anytime and get the prayer I need. And when there's a crisis, they are praying for me, sending messages of encouragement, and quoting passages of Scripture to see me through.

God didn't change the circumstances—this was still a group that was grieving, and I was running a temperature of 102—but he did change the words I spoke and the stories I shared. He carried me on the prayers of my warrior friends and got me through that weekend when I was at my weakest.

Praying God's Word
for Your Physical Health

Jesus went throughout Galilee, teaching in their synagogues, proclaiming the good news of the kingdom, and healing every disease and sickness among the people. (Matt. 4:23)

Jesus, I know that when you were on earth, you were the great healer. You healed the sick, the injured, the sad, and the weary with just a touch or a glance. I pray that you will move likewise in my life. Heal me from my illnesses and injuries and restore my body to health.

He gives strength to the weary
    and increases the power of the weak.
Even youths grow tired and weary,
    and young men stumble and fall;
but those who hope in the LORD
    will renew their strength.
They will soar on wings like eagles;
    they will run and not grow weary,
    they will walk and not be faint.
        (Isa. 40:29–31)

You are my source of strength even when I am too weak to move forward, God. When I am sick or hurt, you come beside me and carry me. I pray that I can rely completely on you when I'm at my weakest and that you will restore me to full strength.

As he went along, he saw a man blind from birth. His disciples asked him, "Rabbi, who sinned, this man or his parents, that he was born blind?"

"Neither this man nor his parents sinned," said Jesus, "but this happened so that the works of God might be displayed in him. As long as it is day, we must do the works of him who sent me. Night is

coming, when no one can work. While I am
in the world, I am the light of the world."
(John 9:1–5)

*O God, you are my healer in every way. There are times
I question whether my own actions have contributed
to my illness or suffering. I worry I'm not praying hard
enough or doing the right things to stay healthy. But
everything that happens is so your greatness can be
displayed. Whether I'm sick or healthy, help me to show
your glory to all who see me, because you are the one
and only light in this dark world.*

After saying this, he spit on the ground,
made some mud with the saliva, and put it
on the man's eyes. "Go," he told him, "wash
in the Pool of Siloam" (this word means
"Sent"). So the man went and washed, and
came home seeing. (John 9:6–7)

*Precious Jesus, you have demonstrated that you work in
miraculous ways to bring forth healing and repentance.
You are the generous giver of good health, and I pray
that you will bless me with that. But I also pray that
I am willing to have you use me in whatever way you
can—in sickness or in health.*

They will be his people, and God himself
will be with them and be their God. "He will
wipe every tear from their eyes. There will
be no more death" or mourning or crying or

pain, for the old order of things has passed away. (Rev. 21:3–4)

God, I am yours! Hold me in your hand and comfort me when my health is failing me. I know you are the Creator and the keeper of my life, and no matter what happens with my health, you are in control. Comfort me with that fact, Lord. I trust you with my health and wait eagerly for the day when there will be no more pain and sickness.

Praying God's Word for Your Emotional and Spiritual Health

For everything God created is good, and nothing is to be rejected if it is received with thanksgiving, because it is consecrated by the word of God and prayer. If you point these things out to the brothers and sisters, you will be a good minister of Christ Jesus, nourished on the truths of the faith and of the good teaching that you have followed. (1 Tim. 4:4–6)

Lord Jesus, help me to receive everything I am given— good or bad—with thanksgiving in my heart because it is given through you. Nourish my soul with your truth and a strong understanding of all that is good so my faith will grow.

Whoever believes in me, as Scripture has
said, rivers of living water will flow from
within them. (John 7:38)

*O God, I believe in you with all of my heart, my mind,
and my soul. Let your living water flow through me so
I am washed clean with your Spirit.*

They have no struggles;
    their bodies are healthy and strong.
They are free from common human burdens;
    they are not plagued by human ills.
Therefore pride is their necklace;
    they clothe themselves with violence.
From their callous hearts comes iniquity;
    their evil imaginations have no limits. . . .
They say, "How would God know?
    Does the Most High know anything?"
      (Ps. 73:4–7, 11)

*O Most High, I know you are omnipotent. You know
all and see all, and you know the state of my soul. God,
I open my heart up to you. Examine me and remove
all iniquities. Take away my pride and my callousness
so I can serve you wholly. Lord, I am fully aware that
my spiritual health is so much more important than my
physical health, so help me to focus on the state of my
soul more often than the state of my body.*

Have nothing to do with godless myths and
old wives' tales; rather, train yourself to be
godly. For physical training is of some value,

but godliness has value for all things, holding promise for both the present life and the
life to come. This is a trustworthy saying
that deserves full acceptance. That is why
we labor and strive, because we have put our
hope in the living God, who is the Savior of
all people, and especially of those who believe. (1 Tim. 4:7–10)

*Lord, help me to be wise in what I say, hear, and believe
so I can become more like you every day. That is my
goal, Jesus. Help me to find ways each day to become
more godly so your love will shine through me.*

You have searched me, LORD,
   and you know me.
You know when I sit and when I rise;
   you perceive my thoughts from afar.
You discern my going out and my lying
      down;
   you are familiar with all my ways.
Before a word is on my tongue
   you, LORD, know it completely.
You hem me in behind and before,
   and you lay your hand upon me.
Such knowledge is too wonderful for me,
   too lofty for me to attain. (Ps. 139:1–6)

*O God, you know me. You know my thoughts. You
know my feelings. You know my strengths. You know
my weaknesses. You know what I'm going to say before
I say it. Search me, O Lord. Reveal to me the dark areas*

174

in my life—the places where this world has a strong-hold. Search me and show me how to walk toward your light, because you are the only path to true spiritual and emotional health.

So whether you eat or drink or whatever you do, do it all for the glory of God.
(1 Cor. 10:31)

Father God, you have chosen me, you have forgiven me, you have restored me, and you have loved me. I thank you for that. Help me to do everything for your glory.

October 31

Dear Friends,

On Thursday, we found out that a lump on my mom's head is a rapidly growing non-small-cell carcinoma (which is normally found in the lungs.) From what we can tell, this is not the kind of cancer you want to get (my mom has had cervical and skin cancer before, but both were highly treatable). We won't know until next week what the prognosis is, but as far as we can tell, it's not good, and the survival rate ranges between 5 and 20 percent. She is not a smoker or a drinker, so it's a mystery why this really rare form of cancer is hitting her.

I am having a hard time compartmentalizing all of this. My mom and I are very close, and a life without her is unimaginable. My dad has also been declining, and the logistics and ramifications are just overwhelming at this moment.

Your prayers would be greatly appreciated. My mom's name is Connie.

The first thing Mom said to me was, "Pray, and get your prayer chain going. Things happen when your people pray." (I keep trying to remind her that God hears her prayers as well, but I don't think she's in a place to hear that at the moment.)

Some of you know my mom and know she would do anything for anyone. She would be the first to bring you a meal or sew you a quilt, and just because I love you, she would too.

Thanks, friends. I appreciate your prayers.

Kathi

November 9

My Most Praying Friends,

For about ten days we thought my mom was diagnosed with lung cancer (non-small-cell carcinoma is almost always a form of lung cancer). However, after a CAT scan, they find no cancer other than the lump (non-small-cell carcinoma) on the side of her head. No cancer is good, but this one can most likely be removed with surgery and is not necessarily a death sentence. We are praising God for his care and love. We are grateful that he has given our mom to us for a little bit more time.

She is having surgery today (Monday for you international friends), and I would appreciate your prayers for my mom, Connie, and our whole family.

In His Grip,
Kathi

November 10

Dear Friends,

The surgery went as well as could be expected, and after sending everything to the lab, we found out that the cancer had not spread to Mom's lymph nodes. She will need to have radiation and chemo, but there is hope that they can get all the cancer.

Kathi

November 11

Dear Friends,

Think about it—a week ago I was trying to imagine what Christmas would be like without my mom, and now all indications are that she will recover. I was hoping I could really experience God's peace in any circumstance, but I am so grateful right now. We just need to wait for her to finish up all of her treatments and see where we're at.

The verse I have been praying this whole time is Philippians 4:7: "And the peace of God, which transcends all understanding, will guard your hearts and your minds in Christ Jesus."

I wanted to experience a peace that even I didn't understand. I prayed that God would guard my heart and mind from believing that he didn't care or wasn't choosing to heal my mom. I wanted to be an example of peace to my mom even when it was hard to imagine doing so.

Kathi

April 10

To all my friends, my prayer warriors, my stretcher bearers, my Aarons and Hurs standing in the battle:

Mom was told that she is cancer-free.

God, we are so undeserving, and so, so grateful.

Kathi

Praying God's Word during a Health Crisis

The year 2008 was a tough time for my family. We had just dealt with a cross-country move from our beloved Colorado based on less-than-positive circumstances. Then, as soon as we arrived in Houston, my fifteen-year-old brother, David, had a brain aneurysm. Actually, two of them. Back to back. The first was six centimeters in his left hemisphere, and the second was 1.5 centimeters in the middle of his brain.

The neurosurgeon who saw my brother at Texas Children's Hospital told my parents that there were only three doctors in the country who could operate on my brother. One surgeon was in Chicago, and a second one was in Phoenix. The third? At Memorial Hermann–Texas Medical Center . . . in Houston. Suddenly our cross-country move seemed a little more fortuitous.

I was raised with the understanding that God answers prayer—in his own way, in his own time, and in his loving perfection. So we prayed for David.

On December 4, 2008, around 10:30 in the morning, David was rushed into surgery to repair the larger of the two aneurysms in his brain. We were hopeful, but just twenty-four hours later, we found out that although my brother had survived the surgery, the doctor had not been able to repair the aneurysm.

Now, David was born with a mild form of cerebral palsy. The left side of his brain was damaged and thus affected the physical mobility of his right side. Because of this, my brother had spent countless hours his entire life fighting for the ability to use his right side normally. The surgery attempted on December 4 was a left-hemisphere artery bypass, but the atrophied left hemisphere of David's brain, as a result of his cerebral palsy, prevented the success of that surgery.

So we had to move on to plan B. Our second surgical option was a coil embolization, which risked the use of David's right arm as well as that of his right leg. One of the things he had worked so hard for his entire life had the probability of being taken from him with one surgery. But we didn't have a choice.

On December 10, around 8:00 in the morning, my brother was prepped for surgery. Again, we prayed. Hourly. This time we prayed Scripture.

> **7:00 a.m.**—For from days of old they have not heard
>   or perceived by ear,
> Nor has the eye seen a God besides You,
> Who acts in behalf of the one who waits for Him.
>   (Isa. 64:4 NASB)
>
> **8:00 a.m.**—Behold, I stand at the door and knock; if
>   anyone hears My voice and opens the door, I will

come in to him and will dine with him, and he
with Me. (Rev. 3:20 NASB)

9:00 a.m.—Remember this, and be assured;
Recall it to mind, you transgressors.
Remember the former things long past,
For I am God, and there is no other;
I am God, and there is no one like Me,
Declaring the end from the beginning,
And from ancient times things which have not been
   done,
Saying, "My purpose will be established,
And I will accomplish all My good pleasure"; . . .
I bring near My righteousness, it is not far off;
And My salvation will not delay
And I will grant salvation in Zion,
And My glory for Israel. (Isa. 46:8–10, 13 NASB)

10:00 a.m.—"Can a woman forget her nursing child
And have no compassion on the son of her womb?
Even these may forget, but I will not forget you.
Behold, I have inscribed you on the palms of My hands;
Your walls are continually before Me.
Your builders hurry;
Your destroyers and devastators
Will depart from you.
Lift up your eyes and look around;
All of them gather together, they come to you.
As I live," declares the LORD,
"You will surely put on all of them as jewels and bind
   them on as a bride." (Isa. 49:15–18 NASB)

11:00 a.m.—Do not fear, for I am with you;
Do not anxiously look about you, for I am your God.

I will strengthen you, surely I will help you,
Surely I will uphold you with My righteous right
hand. (Isa. 41:10 NASB)

12:00 p.m.—For a child will be born to us, a son will
be given to us;
And the government will rest on His shoulders;
And His name will be called Wonderful Counselor,
Mighty God,
Eternal Father, Prince of Peace.
There will be no end to the increase of His govern-
ment or of peace,
On the throne of David and over his kingdom,
To establish it and to uphold it with justice and
righteousness
From then on and forevermore.
The zeal of the Lord of hosts will accomplish this.
(Isa. 9:6–7 NASB)

1:00 p.m.—"Comfort, O comfort My people," says
your God.
"Speak kindly to Jerusalem;
And call out to her, that her warfare has ended,
That her iniquity has been removed,
That she has received of the LORD's hand
Double for all her sins." (Isa. 40:1–2 NASB)

2:00 p.m.—But now, thus says the LORD, your Creator,
O Jacob,
And He who formed you, O Israel,
"Do not fear, for I have redeemed you;
I have called you by name; you are Mine!
When you pass through the waters, I will be with you;
And through the rivers, they will not overflow you.

When you walk through the fire, you will not be
  scorched,
Nor will the flame burn you.
For I am the LORD your God,
The Holy One of Israel, your Savior."
  (Isa. 43:1–3 NASB)

3:00 p.m.—I will go before you and make the rough
  places smooth;
I will shatter the doors of bronze and cut through
  their iron bars.
I will give you the treasures of darkness
And hidden wealth of secret places,
So that you may know that it is I,
The LORD, the God of Israel, who calls you by your
  name. (Isa. 45:2–3 NASB)

4:00 p.m.—Come, let us return to the LORD.
For He has torn us, but He will heal us;
He has wounded us, but He will bandage us.
He will revive us after two days;
He will raise us up on the third day,
That we may live before Him.
So let us know, let us press on to know the LORD.
His going forth is as certain as the dawn;
And He will come to us like the rain,
Like the spring rain watering the earth.
  (Hosea 6:1–3 NASB)

Around 4:00 p.m., one of my friends and I went to Starbucks. On the way back, it began to *snow*. Huge, fluffy, amazing, Colorado-like snowflakes were falling from the sky. It never snows in Houston. *Ever.* I looked at my friend, and he and I both started laughing, overjoyed by snow!

Back in the waiting room, everyone was erupting with the news that it was snowing outside. How *awesome* is our God to give us a simple gift of snow as reassurance that he was with us.

> **5:00 p.m.**—When Israel was a youth I loved him,
> And out of Egypt I called My son.
> The more they called them,
> The more they went from them; . . .
> Yet it is I who taught Ephraim to walk,
> I took them in My arms;
> But they did not know that I healed them.
> I led them with cords of a man, with bonds of love,
> And I became to them as one who lifts the yoke from
>   their jaws;
> And I bent down and fed them. (Hosea 11:1–4 NASB)

At 5:30, the doctor came out with a snippet of news. Six simple words. "I think he will be complete." We rolled those words around in our minds for a while. David will be complete. *Complete.*

> **6:00 p.m.**—Moses said to the people, "Do not fear! Stand by and see the salvation of the LORD which He will accomplish for you today; for the Egyptians whom you have seen today, you will never see them again forever. The LORD will fight for you while you keep silent." (Exod. 14:13–14 NASB)

> **7:00 p.m.**—Moses and the sons of Israel sang this song to the LORD, and said,
> "I will sing to the LORD, for He is highly exalted;
> The horse and its rider He has hurled into the sea.
> The LORD is my strength and song,

And He has become my salvation;
This is my God, and I will praise Him;
My father's God, and I will extol Him.
The Lord is a warrior;
The Lord is His name." (Exod. 15:1–3 NASB)

Finally, after hours of waiting, we were allowed to go speak to David. The first thing I did was tell him to look out the window.

"It's snowing, David!"

"I know," he responded.

"How do you know?" I asked, assuming he was still a little loopy from the anesthesia.

"I prayed for two things last night. First, that after the surgery, I would be whole and complete and would retain the function of my right side. And second, that it would snow. It always snowed on my birthday in Colorado."

God cares—about the prayers of parents for their son's safety, about a community's prayers for a boy to be kept whole and complete throughout his surgery, and even about a boy's prayer for it to snow on his birthday. God doesn't always give us the answers we want when we want them, but he always answers prayer. And his answers are always good.

Barbara

16

Your Mission in Life

Dare to embrace who you are. Dare to do those
weird things you do. Dare to trust God's whispers
into your life more than the demands of the world
around you.

Holley Gerth

A few weeks ago, I met a young doctor with three young
kids who had just quit his job—a very lucrative job, I might
add—to move to Africa and work in a crowded, third world
hospital that serves the poor, the widows, the orphans, and
the oppressed. What an incredible calling—and what a huge
sacrifice!

I have to confess that it would be very hard for me to drop
everything like this man did and move away from my kids,

185

my home, my job, my Starbucks, to go onto the mission field. And while God hasn't called me away from my venti nonfat vanilla lattes—yet, at least—he has called me into a ministry where I am to serve him through serving people on a daily basis. And I pray daily that my heart is always willing to say, "Send me!" and "Use me!" for whatever he asks me to do.

I love that God has called me to minister for him. I love that I have the opportunity to speak into the lives of women around the country through my books and my speaking events. I love watching God use me—yes, little old me—to further his kingdom. But there are days when it takes all I am to pick up that remote and turn off the TV so I can write. And on those days, I turn to God and plead that he'll remind me of the incredible hope I have in him, and that he'll use that hope to inspire me to be a servant leader for him—all day, every day.

That God Would Use You

I was at the women's retreat last weekend (with Morgan Hill Bible Church) and had a funny story I wanted to share with you.

The girls from our small group got together and agreed to do *The Husband Project*—cool, right? Well, after just two days, my husband pulls me aside and says, "You know how when someone goes on a diet and you want to compliment them on how great they look, but you don't want to imply that they looked bad before, so you're caught in a quandary?"

I say, "Yes, but I've only lost two pounds on this diet, so I don't think that's what we're talking about!"

186

He says, "Well, since you got back from that retreat, you have been *really* great! None of the usual stuff is getting under your skin. I know I'm working a ton right now, and you are handling everything so calmly!"

(Reference point: I work part-time, and we have four kids. Our two younger ones, ages nine and twelve, are in full-time sports, our freshman daughter is running for school office—oh, the drama—and our feckless senior son has chosen a $50,000-a-year college. No shortage of stress here.)

Anyhow, obviously I was needing a little attitude check—and his diet analogy had me wanting to laugh out loud. (I kept it in until I could tell my girlfriends.) Just wanted to share that your book is positively impacting my life!

Really enjoyed hearing you speak last weekend.

Cheers,
Kristi

Praying God's Word to Be Used for His Purposes

By the word of the LORD the heavens were
made,
    their starry host by the breath of his
mouth.
He gathers the waters of the sea into jars;
    he puts the deep into storehouses.
Let all the earth fear the LORD;
    let all the people of the world revere him.
For he spoke, and it came to be;
    he commanded, and it stood firm.
The LORD foils the plans of the nations;
    he thwarts the purposes of the peoples.
But the plans of the LORD stand firm forever,

the purposes of his heart through all generations. (Ps. 33:6–11)

Almighty Counselor, you created the stars and the oceans, the summer wildflowers and the beautiful sunrises. You even created me. I stand in awe of your wonderful creation and your plans to use each and every thing you created for the glory of your name. O God, use me for the purposes of your heart so your glory will be revealed in me. Give me the courage to stand up and say, "Use me! Send me!" I willingly submit to your plans and purposes for my life.

The men were amazed and asked, "What kind of man is this? Even the winds and the waves obey him!" (Matt. 8:27)

You are El Shaddai, God Almighty, and when you speak, even the wind and the waves obey. Give me a heart of obedience—a heart that's willing not only to hear your voice but also to obey your commands. Speak clearly to me, God Almighty, and reveal yourself to me through your words.

Do not merely listen to the word, and so deceive yourselves. Do what it says. Anyone who listens to the word but does not do what it says is like someone who looks at his face in a mirror and, after looking at himself, goes away and immediately forgets what he looks like. But whoever looks intently into the perfect law that gives freedom,

and continues in it—not forgetting what
they have heard, but doing it—they will be
blessed in what they do. (James 1:22–25)

*O God, I want to be a doer and not merely a hearer
of your word. Give me the ears to hear and the mind
to understand the freedom that comes from following
you. Keep my mind turned toward you continuously
so I will never forget or overlook your will for my life.*

And whatsoever ye do in word or deed,
do all in the name of the Lord Jesus, giving thanks to God and the Father by him.
(Col. 3:17 KJV)

*Holy Father, everything I do, everything I say, and every-
thing I am is because of you. Thank you for the hope
I have in your Son, Christ Jesus.*

For the Lost around the World

Last August, I heard about a website called www.operation
world.org that encourages Christians to pray for the lost in
different countries around the world. Since then, I've been
attending weekly prayer meetings focused specifically on praying for salvation for the millions of people who have never
heard the gospel around the world. When I first started coming, honestly, it was a time for me to hang out with friends
and get to know people better. God has graciously turned it
into so much more than that.

At some point a few months ago, I realized my prayers were not rooted in compassion; they were done out of habit. When I saw others praying with such fervor and deep concern, I realized I didn't really care about the lost. When talking about and praying for something that should have broken my heart, I was merely apathetic. When I recognized this, I started praying for my prayers. I prayed God would break my heart for the lost just like Jesus's heart was filled with compassion for the crowds. I prayed God would give me a deep love and concern for people. People I have never met and probably never will. People who need God's love and salvation.

God has been so faithful in answering this prayer. When I go to prayer meetings now, it's rare I leave with a dry eye. I love the people of Belarus and the people of Myanmar. Not because I've been there before, not because I've seen what they've gone through or understand their hurts and troubles, but because God has given me a love for them. I love them because God answered my prayers.

Be careful what you pray for. Don't ask for compassion lightly. Compassion has a high cost. It's not easy leading this prayer life. It's not easy never seeing the fruit of your labor. It's not easy knowing that in Bania, India, with a population of over 27 million, no one believes in Jesus. Or in Shaikh, Bangladesh, with a population of over 121 million, not a single one of them has a relationship with God.

But it is worth it to pray. It will be worth it the day I meet people in heaven who are worshiping with me because I prayed for their salvation. It will be worth it when I can eat at the banquet table with a Maldivian on my right and a Belgian on my left who would not have been there without my prayers. God uses prayer to accomplish his will. He will save the lost if you pray for him to send workers into the field, and he will grant you compassion for those who do not know him. I am blessed to be a part of the work he is doing all over the world.

Julianne

Praying God's Word for the Lost

Therefore go and make disciples of all nations, baptizing them in the name of the Father and of the Son and of the Holy Spirit, and teaching them to obey everything I have commanded you. And surely I am with you always, to the very end of the age. (Matt. 28:19–20)

King of Kings, Lord of Lords, you gave us the Great Commission to make disciples of all nations. But I feel so small! My heart aches for the millions who don't know you. Lord, help me to know how to make disciples and to share the good news of your Son with a world that desperately needs him.

Jesus went through all the towns and villages, teaching in their synagogues, proclaiming the good news of the kingdom and healing every disease and sickness. When he saw the crowds, he had compassion on them, because they were harassed and helpless, like sheep without a shepherd. Then he said to his disciples, "The harvest is plentiful but the workers are few. Ask the Lord of the harvest, therefore, to send out workers into his harvest field." (Matt. 9:35–39)

191

Lord Jesus, you are the author and perfecter of my faith. My hope and my joy are in you. I want to share that truth with my family, with my friends, with my neighbors, with my city, and with the world. O great Savior, I am willing. Use me as you will to turn people's hearts toward you.

You who bring good news to Zion,
    go up on a high mountain.
You who bring good news to Jerusalem,
    lift up your voice with a shout,
lift it up, do not be afraid;
    say to the towns of Judah,
    "Here is your God!" (Isa. 40:9)

My deliverer, we live in a dark world, but there is good news! You have come to rescue our world from darkness and to save the lost from destruction. I want to be a disciple maker. Give me the strength, the courage, the stamina, and the desire to share the gospel with those who are hurting. Help me to shout that you are God in everything I do.

How beautiful on the mountains
    are the feet of those who bring good
      news,
who proclaim peace,
    who bring good tidings,
    who proclaim salvation,
who say to Zion,
    "Your God reigns!" (Isa. 52:7)

O Lord, bless the feet of those who bring the wonderful news of the gospel to the lost of the world. Give them the courage to proclaim your salvation and bring the news of your great peace to the ends of the earth. Lord, I pray for the lost. I pray that they will have ears to hear the good news and hearts to turn away from their sin, and that today will be a day of repentance for thousands—even millions—who see the truth and know that God reigns.

17

Your Hope in Christ

He that lives in hope dances without music.

George Herbert

I spend a lot of time thinking and writing about goals. In fact, I wrote a whole book on this topic titled *The Me Project*, which I affectionately call "You Goal Girl." But even though I spend a big part of my day thinking about the future, my perception of what that looks like is constantly changing.

A few years ago, my goals were all about my family and my ministry/career. I had goals for being the best wife, mom, and stepmom I could be. I had goals for the number of books I wanted to write and the size of the audiences I wanted to speak to.

But now my goals are starting to take on a different shape. As I pray and understand God's Word, I continue to realize that there are a lot of different goals God wants me to pay attention to, such as:

- letting my kids know I love them and pray for them, no matter their circumstances;
- praying every day for the ministry God has entrusted me with;
- growing that ministry through connecting with other ministry leaders and encouraging their ministries;
- sponsoring a Compassion International child;
- living a life that is honoring to God in how I spend the time, money, and resources he has given me;
- investing in the marriages of younger couples so they don't have to go through the same pain my husband and I did.

As you pray—both through this book and beyond—I hope that prayer can transform your future and reveal to you the hope that can only be found in Christ.

Praying God's Word for Your Hope in Christ

Open my eyes that I may see
wonderful things in your law. (Ps. 119:18)

I want to see you for who you are, Lord—Creator, Redeemer, Friend. Open my eyes today so I can clearly see you. I pray that you will speak to me through everything I encounter—a beautiful sunset, a quiet evening,

a conversation with a friend, or a hug from a child—so
I can behold your glory in everything.

———————

Like newborn babies, crave pure spiritual
milk, so that by it you may grow up in your
salvation. (1 Pet. 2:2)

I want to please you, my God. Nourish me with your
Word so I will grow to be more like you every day.

———————

May the God of hope fill you with all joy
and peace as you trust in him, so that you
may overflow with hope by the power of the
Holy Spirit. (Rom. 15:13)

The hope I have in you is wonderful, Lord God. I have
joy that comes from knowing you redeemed me from
the mire of my sin and are working in my life to give me
purpose. Help me to be joyful about the incredible gifts
you've given me and to be patient and long-suffering
when things don't go my way. When I struggle, may
my first instinct be to turn to you in prayer. I pray my
life overflows with joy so everyone who sees me will
know I serve the living God.

———————

Your word is a lamp for my feet,
    a light on my path.
I have taken an oath and confirmed it,
    that I will follow your righteous laws.
I have suffered much;

preserve my life, LORD, according to your
  word.
Accept, LORD, the willing praise of my
  mouth,
  and teach me your laws.
Though I constantly take my life in my
  hands,
  I will not forget your law.
The wicked have set a snare for me,
  but I have not strayed from your precepts.
    (Ps. 119:105–10)

*As I stumble through this dark world, O God, your
Word gives me light. I give my life—my family, my
job, my money, my home—all to you, because you are
all I need. I love you, my God! I will never forget that
you are the one who laid the groundwork for my life
long before I was born. I trust you to provide for my
future in a way that's greater than I can even imagine,
so I give you my goals and my future right now. Do
with them as you will so I can live a life that honors
you. Help me not to let anything stand in the way of
the plans you have for me.*

The LORD your God is with you,
  the Mighty Warrior who saves.
He will take great delight in you;
  in his love he will no longer rebuke you,
  but will rejoice over you with singing.
    (Zeph. 3:17)

*Almighty God, you are my Savior. I gladly worship and
praise you because you are the mighty Redeemer of*

your people who has saved me through your incredible
grace. I pray that I can delight you with my life.

I pray that the eyes of your heart may be
enlightened in order that you may know the
hope to which he has called you, the riches of
his glorious inheritance in his holy people,
and his incomparably great power for us
who believe. That power is the same as the
mighty strength he exerted when he raised
Christ from the dead and seated him at his
right hand in the heavenly realms, far above
all rule and authority, power and dominion,
and every name that is invoked, not only in
the present age but also in the one to come.
(Eph. 1:18–21)

Enlighten me, O God! I want to know you on a deeper
and more intimate level. I want to understand the hope
you have given me in a new way. You have granted me
a glorious inheritance through the gift of your Son,
Jesus Christ, and I want to tell the world about this
precious gift! Your power, your love, and your hope are
far greater than any earthly kingdom. I thank you for
choosing me to be your daughter, and I anxiously await
spending eternity worshiping and communing with you.

Praying God's Word for Your Future

This section is based on Psalm 39.

Show me, Lord, my life's end
and the number of my days;

let me know how fleeting my life is.
You have made my days a mere handbreadth;
    the span of my years is as nothing before
      you.
Everyone is but a breath,
    even those who seem secure. (vv. 4–5)

Holy Father, I know this life is temporary. The things that seem so important now—money, success, comfort—just aren't important in light of eternity. Help me to put aside those things that distract me from my life's purpose and, instead, find purpose in you, O God.

Surely everyone goes around like a mere
      phantom;
    in vain they rush about, heaping up
      wealth
    without knowing whose it will finally be.
      (v. 6)

This life is but a breath, and then it will be over. I don't want to spend it in a blur of insignificance. Turn my eyes toward you, heavenly Father, and turn my heart toward your purposes. My hope comes from you and you alone, and I pray that you will remind me of that truth often. My peace and comfort also come only from you, so draw me closer to you every day.

Hear my prayer, LORD,
    listen to my cry for help;
    do not be deaf to my weeping.
I dwell with you as a foreigner,

a stranger, as all my ancestors were.
Look away from me, that I may enjoy life
    again
before I depart and am no more. (vv.
    12–13)

When I pray, you listen, Lord. I am so comforted by that! I am grateful that I am a child of the living God, who not only listens to my cries for help but also comes alongside me and pulls me out of the mire. In you, I have a home. In you, I have a purpose. In you, I have hope for my future. And you are all I need.

Friend, thank you for taking this journey with me. This is holy work we have entered into here. May God bless you and the words of your mouth as you pray his words over your life.

Scripture Index

Kathi Lipp is the author of *Praying God's Word for Your Husband*, *The Husband Project*, *The Me Project*, *The Get Yourself Organized Project*, and several other books. Kathi's articles have appeared in dozens of magazines, and she is a frequent guest on Focus on the Family radio and TV. She and her husband, Roger, are the parents of four young adults in San Jose, California. Kathi shares her story at retreats, conferences, and women's events across the United States. Connect with her at www.KathiLipp.com, or on Facebook or Twitter @KathiLipp.

Meet
Kathi Lipp

Kathi Lipp is a national speaker and author who inspires women to take beneficial action steps in their personal, marital, and spiritual lives.

Connect with Kathi
KathiLipp.com

With warmth and wit, Kathi Lipp shows you not only what a blessing it is to pray boldly for your husband but also the amazing differences you'll see—in him and in yourself—as you pray in full confidence of seeing God-sized results.

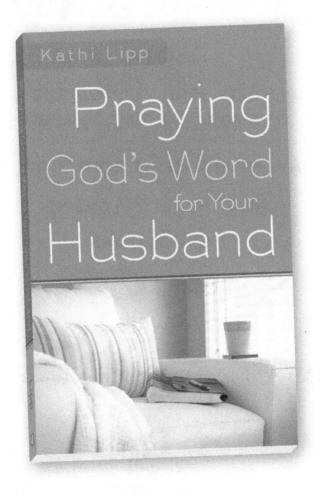

CPSIA information can be obtained
at www.ICGtesting.com
Printed in the USA
BVHW031304120521
607177BV00005B/133

9 780800 720773